CENTERED

CENTERED

BUILDING AFRIKAN REALITIES

Mwalimu K. Bomani Baruti

ISBN: 978-0-9785531-5-9

Akoben House
P.O. Box 10786
Atlanta, Georgia 30310

www.AkobenHouse.com

Cover drawing by Mwalimu K. Bomani Baruti

<u>to</u>

Baba Hannibal Afrik

Intrepid, Centered Jegna

I humbly say medase pa to Odumankoma, the Abosom and the Nananom Nsamanfo who have given me the opportunity to find and work within their center. Every word herein is gratitude and prayer.

Medase to Yaa Mawusi, my innermost sanctuary, who believed this book made sense and made it happen, in spite of the odds. Medowo.

We offer a special medase to our investors, Mama Pamela Kolade Wynn & Baba Elijah Kambon Mann, Baba Morro & Mama Virgestine Sanyang, Baba Baye & Mama Nomzamo Iyanu, and Sisters Amika King and Ife Seshet Robinson, whose selfless support far exceeds any calculable financial value.

I am also especially grateful for the model, insight, assistance and moral support of the Akotos and the Ankobea Society and NationHouse family, Baba Hannibal Afrik, Mama Anana Nyaumu-wi and the New Afrikan Village, the Nyansatumis and the Kwanzaa House family, Kwaw & Bashea Woods, Tony Woods, Haki Ammi & Afua Serwaa, Bro. Mtumwa KMT and the Indaba family, The Nkurobo Mamas and Babas Groups, Asafo Kweku Opare, Baba Makinde Fologbade & Ena Jendayi O. Foluke, Professor Griff, The Habesha Family, Baba Mwaalkebu-lan Akili, Bro. Jon Overton and Family, The Irritated Genie of Soufeese, Sister Rabiyah A. Karmin-Kincey, Brother Joseph & Sister Aleah Gerena and their Ketu and Mama Amanirenis Tafiti and her Asafo. A special medase is given to Brother Akhu Yaw Kamau who selflessly assisted in the design of the graphics. And last, but not least, I am indebted to the presence and power of Mamas Iyaire Atiba, Ayeesha Abdullah (and Baba Kwame Ahmad who is always there when I need him), Marimba Ani and Baba Larry Obadele Williams, who I'm fairly sure do not realize the impact they continue to have on the development of my consciousness of and commitment to the Afrikan Way. This medase extends to a large community of family which consciously and selflessly affords me the opportunity to be as Afrikan as I want to be in the face of this anti-Afrikan onslaught. They are my spiritual, mental and physical shield, sustenance, validation and joy.

Table of Contents

Who For 1

To Be Afrikan 5
   For Those Who Would Lead 8
   On Traditional Ground 11

What is Afrikan Centered? 19
   Reconceptualizing Reality 21
   Whole People 24
   The Circle of Centeredness 26

The Concentric Spheres Model 29
   Zone of Modulation 31
   Medial Zone 33
   Innermost Sanctuary 34
   Final Thoughts 37
   The Qualification 42

"Afrkan" Psychologies 41
   A Typology of People of Afrikan Ascent 47
      Afrikan Warrior Scholars 47
      Nationalist Intellectualizers 47
      Humanist Reactors 48
      Lost Souls 48
      Rejecters 49
      Sympathetic (Apologetic) Proselytizers 49
      Apathetic Proselytizers 50
      Hateful Eunuchs 50
      Passive (apolitical) negroes 50
      Active (calculating) negroes 51
      Nonblacks 51
      Crossovers/Passers 52
   Another Useful Typology 52

The "New" Afrikan 59
   True ReAfrikanization 62
      Traditions 69
      Technology..70
   Healing Internal Ruptures...71
   The Question of All-Inclusiveness 76
      The New Vanguard 82
   Collective Villages...84
   Study and Application...85
   Progress..98

Building Family Within 103
   Centered Complementarity 105
   Critical Capacity...108
   Morale 110
   Grounded 113
      Immeasurable Evil...118
   Ujamma 122
   Fihankra 127

The Role of Elders 133

Conclusion 143

<u>Who For</u>

If you are parents of worth and wisdom, train your children so that they will be pleasing to God. And if they do what is right, following your example, and handle your affairs as they should, do for them all that is good. For they are begotten of your own heart and soul. Therefore, separate not your heart from them. But if they fail to follow your course, oppose your will, reject all counsel, and set their mouth in motion with vile words, then drive them away. For they are not your children and were not born for you. Those who are guided do not go wrong, but those who willfully lose their way will not find a straight course.

Ptah Hotep

As with every book written, this is a political discussion. I make no claims to neutrality or western notions of objectivity. No sane soldier does.

We are at war. There is friend and there is foe. There are warriors and there are cowards. In the end, there must be liberation or obliteration.

This is a warrior's handbook, specifically designed for Afrikan centered warrior scholars,[1] both male and female, who understand what comes with claiming ownership of an

1

uncompromising commitment rooted in war. It is for those of us who are courageous enough to see where we have been and our condition in this reality through the eyes of our strongest Ancestors. And, it is for those Afrikans who, from this understanding, know that it is we who must fight, using every means and energy at our disposal, to regain control over ourstory, our Way[2] and our destiny.

This book is no place for individualists. Those eternally committed to eureason[3] and their europeanisms[4] should go elsewhere for intellectual stimulation or, rather, deadening. Individuals dedicated to the practice, promotion and defense of sexual misidentification, interracialism, subintegration, and the pacification of Afrikan males and masculinization of Afrikan females would be much better off continuing to blindly listen to the host of readily available confused personalities for culturally misoriented sustenance.

This book is not about how we all can get along, or even how all Afrikans can get along. Neither is a possibility in this reality, if Afrikans with a wholesome, righteously enraged, knowing vision become spiritually and psychologically empowered. A conscious people does not harbor the voice or seeds of treason ("their own destruction") within.

Be that as it may, the answer to the question of us all getting along is obvious to warrior scholars and something I have addressed thoroughly in previous books. Afrikans who choose to ignore this, who follow the europhilic negro and lost soul leaders for whatever reason, get what they deserve. Enough is enough.

Know that what goes around comes around. Know that our most ancient of Ancestors are most correct. Know that there were no negroes among our Ancestors in ancient times. There was nothing then to have created them.

With this said, we readily acknowledge that this book is written for a particular audience. It is a contribution to the idea of a self-defining, self-empowered nation of Afrikan people, nothing less. Therefore, it is not written for those among us who:

1) are full of loathing self-hatred, want to create some new, hybrid, colorless, acceptable, i.e., open-(to European imperatives)-minded, person through an impossible blending of the Afrikan with the European or a more realistic melding of the Afrikan into and under the European,

2) fear invisibility more than their own mirror image and, if compelled, want to be Afrikan in name only, i.e., superficially through wearing their hair natural and draping themselves in traditional attire, and maybe even reading some of our classics, but whose heart and mind still lie in the european ideal – people who would more properly be called "safe" or "feel good" Afrikans, or

3) are tortured by their own foolishness in the face of overwhelming truth, want to use a knowledge of Afrikan traditions, ourstorical glories and integration-focused, imitative "Black Firsts"[5] to buttress their fragile egos so they can march into whiteness without being too psychologically damaged.

On the other hand, this book is specifically for Afrikans who:

1) believe in the ingenuity, humility, resilience, integrity and truth of our Ancestors; who believe in the inviolability and incomparability of Afrikan people and the Afrikan person,

2) see the corruptive, insane, anti-Afrikan nature of the western social and cultural wasteland and know that it is a physical, spiritual and psychological deathtrap for Afrikans who want to be their human selves, and

3) understand that there should not be a contradiction between what we say and do, and that this sacred connection defines the quality of our character and the level of our humanity.

What we do, how we practice life, how we speak to ourselves and others, and what we think about how we speak and act must be one. It must be fully in sync with an Afrikan centered interpretation of reality. Otherwise, we are not Afrikan at heart.

To Be Afrikan

It has been said by many wise and learned people that the descendants of the Afrikans who were kidnapped and brought to the Americas where they were enslaved and oppressed need to realize who they are. It is amazing that so many rich and powerful people have spent so much time, money and energy in order to keep us from realizing and understanding our Afrikanity. This is made more amazing when we see descriptions of us written in "mainstream" media, like, "powerless minority" and "at-risk". If we are so powerless and endangered, why are they expending so many resources to keep a "self checked" people down. They apparently know something about us that we don't know. The reawakening of our Afrikan selves is essential to our survival. Although culture is the battlefield and we do indeed face terminal cultural dissociation because of the theft and reassignment of our culture, we also face physical extinction. A people without a culture or without a means of holding on to their culture is threatened by their elimination from the face of the earth. It means nothing if phenotypically Afrikan people continue to exist physically if they have been separated from their own identities and culture. If we look at the plight of Afrikan people, on the Afrikan continent and in the Diaspora, trying to adapt to alien cultures and value systems, the danger of trying to be what we aren't should become obvious.

Burnett Kwadwo Gallman

When one listens, one learns. And when we listen

carefully to what a number of Afrikans have to say about what it means to truly be Afrikan, a very important, extremely critical fact stands out. Many Afrikans do not have a clear understanding of just what it means to be Afrikan.

Certainly, some of us do plainly see who we must be. But many remain lost. They blindly grope their way through libraries of literature and myriad voices, hoping to stumble upon truth and suddenly wake from the nightmare of their confusion and unconstructively channeled rage into a clearer view of reality and self.

Others, having been thoroughly brainwashed by the white supremacist propagating culture to which they have now fully succumbed, believe that being Afrikan is only an act, a show, that it is only another way of being individually unique, but not altogether different from being European. To them, being Afrikan is simply an optional, idiosyncratic choice. They see it as only another or alternative way of pretending to be different from Europeans through dress, diet or a rhetoric that has no more substance than the lies of those they dutifully mimic.

Quite a few of those who swim on the surface of being Afrikan have simply exchanged the politics of a blatantly anti-Afrikan propaganda for a seemingly less self-hating one, which allows them to believe that, by turning a deaf ear and blind eye to a determined enemy, they will be saved from its destructive forces. Still others, overwhelmed by the white noise, simply give up on the possibility of their Afrikan selves before they even try.

But do not be thrown by any of their confusions. Being Afrikan is not an act. It is not a show or charade. And it is definitely not something we dress up in to hide our racial scars while they continue to fester beyond the point of healing. To be Afrikan is a Way of thinking, doing, feeling and speaking that steadily and uncompromisingly moves us along the already well-trodden paths of our ancestors. It is to become intimately acquainted with ancestral truth to the point where we and it become one.

Neither should we feel any discomfort in taking uncompromising stands in all areas of life. There is an unmistakable difference between being intolerant and being resolute. Intolerance, something our Ancestors abhorred and those who have historically embraced it the most are now trying to convince us that we must move away from in order to embrace their abnormalities as normal,[6] is an absence of the acceptance of others or their unique ways, except as they can be sub-absorbed, without disruption, into yours.

Being uncompromising is to refuse to alter one's people's view of reality in the face of forces trying to do just that. It is an indicator of having a strong, righteous conviction, of knowing that our Ancestors are correct and acting powerfully to defend our right to be them, regardless of the odds against us.

While the knowledge of what it means to be Afrikan patiently awaits us just below the surface of our assaulted consciousness, it cannot be tapped into without the right psychological triggers. We must know that it exists, that it is critical to our development as thinking Afrikans, that we must look inward for it and, then, outward from within it. Until that awakening occurs, we remain ignorant of self.

Ignorance means that you are unaware of something's existence, not simply that you do not know it well. Not knowing, without a desire not to know, is neither a character flaw nor a statement about one's intelligence or intellectual ability. Ignorance simply indicates that there is something unknown to the individual due to a lack of exposure or awareness. This is quite different from stupidity where, in the context of this discussion, you know truth, but you allow your loyalty to another's way and/or fear of reprisal from thinking against another's way, to prevent you from acting on what you have learned.

Even though an unconscious ignorance of self is to be expected for most Afrikans living in the western cultural chaos, it should not be expected among Afrikans who have seriously undertaken a study and practice of the Way of our Ancestors. It's almost ironic that knowing what it means to be Afrikan is such a simple, but remarkably consequential factor for realizing ourselves, yet passing this thought on is so often overlooked by some of the warrior scholars who are earnestly working to help educate our community.   No lesson should come before this.

This grave oversight is still plainly evident within many of us who have already consciously decided that we are not and do not, in any way, want to be europeanized.   People at war do not hide the acts and nature of their enemy from their children for fear that they may respond to this knowledge with a righteous rage.   That is their hope.

If we are to liberate our minds and people from a life of chronic, debilitating mentacide,[7] we must study its causes and consequences.   Yet, clear-sightedness about our enemy (within and without) is no guarantee that we will automatically recognize and follow an independently empowering Afrikan path.   So many of us know what we do not want, but are still unaware of what we should want or how to get there.   We knowingly run from an anti-Afrikan insanity.   However, we do so without conscious direction.   We remain unfamiliar, at a most basic, working, practical level, with the Afrikan Way, a way understood and practiced by those who have consciously placed themselves within our Center.

For Those Who Would Lead

For those of us who would lead, not having explained our traditional Way in as broad and uncomplicated a way as possible to aspiring warrior scholars, first, is an oversight of great consequence.   It becomes a progressively crippling flaw in the critical thinking among educators in a community diligently working to explain who we are to us and what we should be doing as Afrikans.   No matter the quality of the intent, it is a dangerous disservice and a serious statement of intellectual neglect to overlook the foundations of traditional Afrikan culture and society when communicating a nationbuilding[8] vision to the inquisitive in our family.

We have inherited deeply rooted psychological wounds. And although some of us have a heightened awareness, a burning eagerness to learn and, often, an impatience to righteously confront the sources of our ongoing destruction, we must learn and vent correctly so as not to further damage ourselves and give advantage to those who see us as their food and tools. As grassroots educators,[9] we are often driven to skip over the cultural mind of Afrika and immediately go down a list of glorious and worthy ancient "firsts." Some of us even feel compelled to introduce rehashed, pacifying ideas of reform and subintegration oriented plans which will inevitably drive our listeners even farther back into the insanity they so desperately hope to escape.

Without thinking, we engage in the rhetoric of "firsts" because this is what we have been taught that we need to be "successful." But these accomplishments are simply the icing on a grand, many layered cake, baked well before contact with Europeans or Arabs. We first need to rebuild our knowledge of this solid cake. We need to know that our "greatest stories and traditions lie far beyond these shores in both time and space."[10] We need to know our Way.

Knowing our Way helps us to understand why we did what we did and why we were so phenomenal at it. With that science under our belts we can successfully go about the business of a systematic self-discovery and serious nationbuilding *supported* with politically astute selections of those who reflect our genius.[11]

Seasoned warrior scholars often wrongly assume that a common, elemental understanding of the character and quality of the traditions which ourstorically define and characterize Afrikans as Afrikans is somehow inherently known by all who have decided to search out, internalize and follow them. It never occurs to some of even the most serious of us who have dedicated our lives to helping build more like us that this crucial intellectual, psychological and emotional base is incomplete or, for all revolutionary intents and purposes, absent from many a neophyte's understanding of where we are trying to go. We tend to forget that every Afrikan must be his own head so that, dispersed or collectively, we continue to move toward our group's ReAfrikanization.[12] Even those among us who know that this basic understanding of who we inherently are must be in place before the politics of our movements toward becoming Afrikan can be intelligently and consciously decided upon can miss the importance of passing this vital knowledge on before going into specific or isolated details of ourstory.

Nonetheless, having a personal memory of the mentacidal vacuum created in the Afrikan's consciousness by this anti-Afrikan insanity, it should be common sense that most "neophytes" are not acquainted with this knowledge. We must remember that what is taken as given to those of us who have traveled this path for a while is no more typical among those who have just begun this journey than it was for us when we began it.   Some things require explanation.

For a people who are spiritually, culturally, mentally and physically adrift, nearly completely lost in a sea of insanity, fighting to find our way home, so many times already deceived by faulty life jackets and floatation devices, limited, inverted knowledge of navigation or the stars and taunting rescue mirages, all the while hunted by enemy search boats on constant patrol in the amniotic waters around our asili[13] and already infested by the sharks that hunted and fed on our Ancestors, rescue is needed.

Without this key understanding of who we are when whole, they, like most of us initially, run to and fro from club to organization, from church to mosque to temple, from lectures to guru to intellectual, from quack to medicine man to wholistic healer, from community to collective to individual islands, from city to city in one state to another, graduating to the Continent, moving still further on from one continent to another searching for "home." They search unanchored in traditional ground, unsure of the whole path. Nothing makes them whole.

We must know the core of our ancestors' traditions in order to operate independently as Afrikans wherever we are, whether those we look to for knowledge are still physically around or not. It is that autonomous Afrikan centered consciousness that we, as individuals, need to possess in order to successfully wage this war for our sanity. As a people, we need Afrikans who can stand both alone and with our communities as warriors.

It is the framework for solving this problem of implanted ignorance about what it truly means to be Afrikan among awakening Afrikans that we must provide. Even though most of us are still firmly held captive in yurugu's[14] reality, those with the audacity, capacity[15] and need must be equipped with the means to rise above whiteness. And it is not as difficult a task as most would imagine. As guides, jenoch,[16] elders, as practical, active, accountable resources to these budding "Sankofans,"[17] all we need do is take the time to remember what we did not know, and now wished we had, when we decided to walk in the footsteps of our Ancestors.[18]

As it was with us, all it requires is that they be given a basic description and the cardinal principles and definitions that form the core of our Way as a people. Then, to that, we only need provide whatever guidance they ask as to where to go from there for even deeper ReAfrikanizing study. If they are disciplined, observant and resolute, they will find their way as we did.

On Traditional Ground

Because of Afrikan tradition's severe beating at the exclusivist hands of an aspiring imperialist eurosupremacy, we must have a discussion of its relevance for those who actually aspire to be Afrikan. We must hash out the arguments of whether or not we can apply a traditional way of living to this day's world/reality. We must realistically asses if, how and where we can use the traditional Afrikan model as the core foundational tool for patterning our present and future thought, discussions and behavior here and globally.

Many among us will say that you cannot live in the past, that it must be "let go" of because that was then and this is now, that traditional ways died for good reason. They feed us images of dirty, deprived, superstitious, scantily clad or naked, hungry, uneducated, abused, deserted Afrikan bodies caught somewhere between an animalistic barbarity and innocent backwardness suggested as being of their own doing. They tell us that this is what remains of people when they refuse to move "forward." This is supposed to be the result when a people cannot adjust to or keep pace with change (a phenomenon eurocentric science calls a lack of modernity). They become lost in the limbo of another world, a traditional one, that has no place in this one.

Sadly, the tradition that comes to mind for most of us when we think of our Motherland is that which has been manufactured and circulated by european invaders and their minions during the period of our colonization/direct captivity by them. This is a false, european-imposed traditionalism. In only very limited ways does it reflect the tradition we, as Afrikans, should hold in esteem. It is a severely distorted culture, held up as us but suspended between who we were and can return to. Any culture, like dammed water cut off from its source, stagnates if the dynamic life which feeds and moves it dies. This sham of cultural subsistence was not that of our Ancestors.[19]

In this falsified tradition, an imitative patriarchy of privilege existed which defined men as women's superiors and possessors. In this imposed, artificial social environment, royalty was made arrogant and exploitative, and graft became normalized.   Important rituals became petty tools for manipulating the dispossessed; spirituality grew into a means of scaring the uninitiated into submission and willful destitution, and names carried less and less meaning and power. In this "traditional" setting, everything Afrikan was suspect and targeted for obliteration to make room for others' traditions.

Though this gross misrepresentation is the "tradition" Afrikans in flight from self speak of when trying to belittle our origins, it is not the tradition of which knowledgeable Afrikan warrior scholars speak. As with so many other things aliens and the mentacidal speak of as Afrikan without basis in fact, this was never us. What we speak of as Afrikan tradition is what was actually practiced and lived before the arrival of destroyers. It is only as the result of a protracted, reactive response to an unremitting, total, dehumanizing oppression, that what would otherwise be called tradition, has lost its elasticity, dynamism and human essence and become petrified in its colonized underdevelopment. And though seemingly lost to those without focus, undefiled tradition is the greatest evidence of who we are and the source of our social and cultural identify.

Those who venerate our enemy's way would further have us believe that modern European society is the only possible human reality, the only viable contemporary existence. Twisted into such a deformed, self-debasing misorientation forces us to believe that european culture and society are the logical direction in the inevitable social evolution of the human enterprise. As with every other western evolutionary model, this mentality naturally associates that which comes last or, rather, that which remains standing on top after the many survival of the fittest battles for supremacy, with the best of all human possibilities.[20]

Buying into this social evolutionary model inevitably leads us to accept that it is only because of the rise of the ultra-rational, despiritualized[21] European production machine that personal freedoms can be truly enjoyed and our every material want so easily satisfied.   If we balk without the reason of our Ancestors and do not understand the systematic manufacture of wants,[22] and these wants into needs, or the level of resource exploitation demanded by the creation and satisfaction of these newfound "needs," Europeans readily present evidence of their advances using heart-wrenching images of what happens to those of us who go against their way.   For most of us, all they need do is tell us to look around at the grand things, images, titles, offices and other "blessings" they have given us to enjoy. For the gullible, the argument is sealed when they contrast that "privilege" with the condition of Afrikans living on the fringes of Yurugu's benevolence and beyond the magnanimity of their empire.   They steer our ignorance and fear in the direction of believing that the disadvantage and longing of these dispossessed souls would also be ours, if not for their genius and generosity.[23]   Even in the face of its incredible assemblage of catastrophic, irresolvable problems, we are left but to assume that western society's material advantages and social privileges (opportunities for upward mobility) outweigh its inherent faults and contradictions.

Some vanquished Afrikans even try to pretend that this culture is really progressing toward a new sympathetic, peaceful, finally humane age, a newfound humanity.   Blindly forgetful of today and yesterday, these uprooted, fractured individuals put all their energy into acting as if this insanity is some form of sanity.   Having bought the european lie of progressive evolutionism, they see western society as having fully arrived from a callous, violent, unscientific barbarism to an enlightened, reformed civilization. [24]   They believe these haughty children have learned to be considerate adults.

Only mentacidal Afrikans try to pretend this sickness is normal.   And, not only do they act as if it is to be expected, but also like it is the best condition we have ever been in or could hope to be in at this point in "our" evolution.   They try to convince themselves that this situation is somehow ordinary, that it is not as ugly or devastatingly dehumanizing as it is.   If they are not successful in deluding themselves into this fatal fantasy, they work to convince themselves that we, hand in hand with Yurugu, are steadily overcoming all obstacles in "our" movement toward normalcy.

Others of us, however, have not completely lost our Afrikan minds. We have developed and followed theories and programs designed to correct for these faults and contradictions inherent in eurocentric thinking. Some have even been courageous enough to dare to think to create an independent reality outside of this pale, dead matrix. But more have sought to reform it or change it into a more egalitarian state without modifying its heart. As might be expected, the latter have also contributed to the movement of Afrikan people toward a deeper subassimilation [25] into this alien paradigm called european society. For, while their "sacrifices" have allowed us access to more of the trappings of a materialistic ethic, these things have made us increasingly more oblivious to our systematic exploitation. Their conscious efforts, however "kindly intentioned," have steadily moved us away from the Way of our Ancestors and into a more and more binding orbit around Yurugu's.

The independent efforts of those who operate in sync with the rhythm of our Afrikan center are the only ones which have truly kept us close to home. Their feats of incredible s/heroism in the face of enemies constantly circling about and often seemingly permanently entrenched can be judged as no less than phenomenal. Altruistic nationalism is a dauntless balancing act between individual survival and living on the militarized fault line, which could only be performed by those of us who refuse to accept our Ancestors as simply the pathetic recipients of the tolerance of a white supremacy seemingly divinely ordained to mold and furnish the needs and destiny of a humanity lost to order.

Nationbuilders all, these s/heroes' efforts have been consistently grounded in Afrikan tradition in the asilic foundations of Afrikan people. They have been nationalist in political orientation,[26] Pan Afrikan in ideological formation, definition and outreach. The importance of tradition in grounding a people in their culture and possibilities is not questioned by these few, proud, ancient spirits. The only question these workers have been forced to pause to answer is how to continue standing in face of a horrific, ongoing, anti-Afrikan assault to our being. As models of sacrifice and liberation, their only frustration comes from figuring out how to better convince Afrikan people to love, be and empower themselves.

ReAfrikanization and nationbuilding transform Afrikans back into themselves and their power. As we work toward this state of being we have to bear in mind that transformation is a process or, rather, part of a process or stage in redevelopment. It characterizes the ourstorical pattern of a cycle that is returning us to ourselves. And, because this is true, we learn through the challenges this process brings that we cannot allow the catastrophic rupture in this life-affirming cycle to repeat itself.

Kwame Agyei Akoto tells us there are seven phases in the cycle Afrikans are experiencing.[27] In order from our auspicious beginnings to our visionary return to it, they are: (1) Cultural Coherency and Order, (2) Cultural Deterioration, (3) Defeat and Humiliation, (4) Cultural Entropy and Chaos, (5) Rebirth, (6) Cultural Reconstruction and (7) New Order.

We have already gone through the first five. We once existed in a state of Ma'at, in harmony with the Universe and each other. Our decline has been identified with the invading presence of others, skilled in disorder and devoid of civilization, but welcomed into our xenophilic hearts, and our gradual, forced, mistaken submission to their iniquitous, spiritless ways. Physical, mental, spiritual, cultural devastation followed in rapid succession, for over 3,000 years raining a hell storm of fragmentation, poverty and powerlessness upon our people, giving many of us cause to lose memory. This is the climax of the rupture.

Pushed down beyond belief, there were still those among us who refused to accept others' lies about our natural state. Following a distinguished tradition of resilience, we rose over and over again. We uncovered and relearned what was more than skin deep, as well as what secrets our resplendently melaninated skin held.

From this milestone, we began to reclaim what was inherently ours. We studied and built institutions modeled in the true spirit of our Ancestors. We did this even in the face of continuing great confusion among our own and the systematic work of our would be destroyers against us. We can trace all of these phases ourstorically and, today, assess the degree of the retention of the effects from each one.

I would agree with Akoto that we are currently in the sixth phase, that point of full cultural awakening among an almost destroyed people where they gather the best, most functional whole of their original culture around themselves, albeit in a global situation drastically altered from the time when they were one. Our rebirth into who we are gave rise to this realization and the force of who we are galvanized us to save ourselves from a corrupted, self-hatred. The best of us have realized that culture is the key to sustaining the momentum of this awakening until we can see no other way than that of our Ancestors.

I would also concur that we have yet to come into a "New Order." This requires us to recreate a reality based on the oneness of Afrikan people. And this demands that we defend and advance all that which is Afrikan wherever Afrikan people work, eat, love, sleep and think. Although yet to arrive, the time is on the horizon when we respect and honor ourselves enough to return to the world stage fully empowered, as the people we naturally are.

At the individual level, the normalized, westernized ideas of superindividualism, exaggerated, deceit-fostering personal freedoms, and our inbred inability to distinguish needs from wants, have proven to be the greatest roadblocks to

ReAfrikanization for so many of our people. For even if extreme individualism were an Afrikan option it would not work within the confines of an alienating culture where a highly perfected individualism can lead Afrikan people nowhere, except deeper into that soulless chaos. Finding correct and effective ways of solving these problems as Afrikans is critical to gaining a broader base of Afrikans who find reason to embrace and implement our most ancient and uncontaminated traditions.

Sadly, though, this is not foremost among the aspirations of most Afrikan scholars. It never ceases to amaze me how people taking the intellectual low road to what is and is not Afrikan always seem to find a way to stop short of seeking our truth as it existed before the physical and cultural invasion of our people by others to the periods when we were solely Afrikan. Interestingly, many in the modern PanAfrikanist school fit this bill. Yes, the long term goal for these shallow thinkers is the elevation of Afrikan people globally. But this is only sought after in order to be finally visible as human beings to Europeans in the effort to have them want to live with us in peace. All this is so that we can convince ourselves that race is no longer an issue in their eyes.

These same confused Afrikan spokespeople will do all in their power to convince us that the situation we now find ourselves battling is the failing (if we accept that there has been a failure) of cultural nationalists who attempt to use our traditional way as a model of our present and future endeavors. But cultural nationalism forms the foundation of all people who gain hold of their power.

Powerfully thinking people have *always*, because they know that the trial and error of their ancestors found the way that was correct for them, returned to themselves in defining themselves. They never lose sight of their original reality, their proven enemies and their future. They never lose sight of home. None leave their ancestors or way behind on the road to full empowerment.

What is Afrikan Centered?

Africa is our center of gravity, our cultural and spiritual mother and father, our beating heart, no matter where we live on the face of this earth.

John Henrik Clarke

Here, we need to address the questions of both what is "Afrikan centered" and of where that center is. Confusion is rife in our community with the greater portion of answers given for both. In fact, "Afrikan centered" has become a catch-all designation, much the way "Black" did. Any and everybody with a predominately, or even significant, Afrikan student body, workforce, constituency or following can call themselves Afrikan, even when they openly admit that any Afrikan centering is far to the periphery of, or totally antithetical to, what they do or promote.

As the label Afrikan centered becomes more diluted, in terms of what it represents, the more it becomes over- and misused. The term has become politically neutralized. And, as more of us have become attracted to this term, more of us seeking mainstreamed or otherwise compromised clients or an unqualified, unaccountable (to Afrikan people) popularity have self-interestedly abused it.

It can be expected that predominantly european, as well as eurocentric negro and lost soul, organizations, will place "African centered" in their title or description, without challenge or effective censorship from the Afrikan community.

So many of us are searching for any sign that Europeans don't hate us anymore that any effort by Yurugu to commandeer more of our essence is credible evidence of their love.

Regardless, the immediate goal of Afrikan warrior scholars should be to move toward the autonomous designation of Afrikan, even though it cannot be our final identification.[28] We cannot be upset over our children calling themselves "niggas" as a term of endearment when we are not taking the steps to be more correct in naming ourselves in an ourstorically grounded way.

With this said, in answering the question of *what* Afrikan centered is, we would say that to be Afrikan centered is to be grounded in a working knowledge of our uncompromised Afrikan traditions. It is to be crystal clear about the fact that our traditions are best for us, in practical and ideal terms. It is to know that we are Afrikan and, for this reason, we should interpret the world through the Universe-based, humanistic understanding of our ancestors. It is to think about and act on all planes of reality as they would, knowing that we are they.

Being centered is to be in sync with the Afrikan Way, which refers to the manner in which Afrikans have traditionally interpreted and acted in this world (i.e., before european and arab contamination). It is reflected in our evolved cultural imperatives and the spiritual, psychological and physical manifestations in which we naturally immerse ourselves. It is reflected in that common core of values, beliefs and practices that run through all Afrikan ethnic groups.[29]

While necessarily aware of others' traditions, which in this reality is a critical knowledge allowing one to make distinctions between what we are and the lesser humans others want us to be, awareness of the what and why of our Ancestors' wisdom, beliefs, material creations, institutions, interpretations of reality, cosmology and relations with others come first for the Afrikan centered individual. The knowledge that we are our Ancestors is enough to know that their traditions are ours. We respect ourselves when, and only when, we respect our

Ancestors. We are ourselves when, and only when, we think and act in the spirit and Way of our Ancestors.

The Afrikan centered warrior scholar thinks, speaks and acts in the tradition of our Ancestors but does so aware of where we are and why we are here. So, while in private and/or in the presence of others of equal or greater understanding, we think and speak differently than when in the presence of those with no Afrikan understanding or who are resolutely anti-Afrikan. We know this is not an Afrikan society and do not waste time trying to turn something European, Arab or Asian into something Afrikan. We firmly stand on our source.

Reconceptualizing Reality

Becoming Afrikan centered thinkers requires that we reconceptualize our reality in Afrikan terms and ways of knowing and doing. As a function of correctly defining and acting as Afrikans, our reality naturally changes. Power shifts and balance returns. It is a process of conscious visualization and activation. Because we think so, it becomes so.

Reconceptualization is the process of searching out and/or creating more appropriate terms and, especially, meanings to terms that better fit the logically self-interested, nationbuilding politics of our research and agenda. In refusing to accept being bound by others' self-serving, anti-Afrikan interpretation of reality, we are creating, and applying in our daily lives, a "language of resistance."

Because it is not necessary to spend years of study learning about all of the facets and arguments involved in understanding exactly what is meant by most of these Afrikan centered definitions, this book provides short versions of an otherwise lengthy, drawn out, intellectualized scholarly analysis of basic sociological concepts. As we begin, though, we should be aware that sociology, like every other discipline, is not of European origin.[30]

As with all concepts, our reconceptualizations have full political intent. Our keen awareness of this fact has forced us to explain these terms specifically as they apply to Afrikan centered thinkers and the Afrikan reality we are intent on remaking in the image of our Ancestors. As people guided by a liberating vision, it is imperative that we identify, define and develop those aspects of culture most relevant to our ReAfrikanized nationbuilding. Done together, we reconceptualize our reality into that of powerful, focused warrior scholars.

Except in passing or in a general way, our discussion of what each reconceptualization means and consists of is not meant to explain the obvious or superficial. Each reconceptualized phenomenon, as a social entity, a social creation identified with the human intellect, genius, capacity and will to make the natural and social environment into what we ideally imagine, has a basic definition. These definitions have an actively politically conscious Afrikan center and are strictly for the edification and benefit of Afrikan people.

It should also be noted that this is not an introduction to these concepts. It should be considered a *re*introduction to the primary, common principles, attributes and practical manifestations of the Afrikan Way because they have been here as long as we have, and we once lived them as our own. If all that we have ever been is always with us, only unrecognized if we have forgotten who we are and have always been, then we cannot be introduced to what we already know.

The Way of which these words speak is not new to us. It never was new to us. We have always been there. We just need remembrance.

We are only confused because we have allowed others, from inside and outside our family, to convince us that it is not within us to be Afrikan and that we should accept the decrepit abyss around us now as our only home. We are only confused because we have allowed others, within [31] and without, to convince us that we are too divided from each other and distant from our origins to begin to rebuild, here and now, what we were and are still. Our confusion has led us to submit to the possibility that the traditional Afrikan reality we are searching for is merely a figment of our imagination, a childish fantasy world that never did and never can exist.

Yet, if we think about accepting this debilitating evaluation of our potential, we will not be able to see an evident contradiction. We will look around and still not be able to see that we were brought to this place to do the impossible. The odds ourstorically placed against us and our survival nonetheless will elude our sight. We will remain oblivious to a story telling of the victorious struggle against what no other people have come close to surviving if we do not see and believe we are Afrikan. What we believe we cannot do springs from nothing more than our confusion over who we are and the power of the Afrikan mind. The critical lesson here is that "people who want power, but who don't know what power is, don't get it."[32]

Nothing is impossible for Afrikans with the will to do what is necessary and a clear understanding of what needs to be done. We only need to have a fearless, uncompromising vision of what a traditional Afrikan world would have to be like in today's reality to give our thoughts and actions that true aim. We have only to return to what already exists inside us. It has gone nowhere. We have been, are now and always will be Afrikan. No power on this earth can, and no benign power in the Universe would ever think to, change that.

Many of us are earnestly searching for our original selves. We have too long felt the discomfort of being in a place that pulls us against our spirit. And we have discovered that to find our Way we must look deeply back into ourselves to see what our true self is at all times. Through trial and error we have learned that "to go back to tradition is the first step forward," something our ancestors have always known. The concepts of Sankofa[33] and Kebuka,[34] of returning to origins to find contemporary direction, are creations of their genius.

So, here, for those of us forcibly distanced from ourselves generations ago, we are only reintroducing ourselves to the reason and order we originally created for ourselves. With that said, what we are doing is simply presenting a moderately in-depth discussion of how uncontaminated Afrikan people traditionally think and act.

Whole People

Our political perspective as Afrikans is critically important in reconceptualizing and implementing definitions that are so vital for our survival as human beings. We are an Afrikan people, frustrated externally and internally, at war for the control and sustainability of our motherland and the lineages of her children subsisting in the diasporic communities we were taken to against our will and otherwise. We are a people long suffering the pain of manufactured illnesses, fighting for gratification, contentment and happiness. We are a dispossessed people standing on the verge of forgetfulness, fighting for our empowerment as a whole people. We are a "conceptually incarcerated" [35] people on the verge of exhaustion and brink of vanquishment, fighting for the reason and will to return to, and keep ourselves at, our center. Regardless of obstacles, though, we, the warrior scholars of Afrikan people, are PanAfrikan cultural nationalist socialists[36] determined to unite Afrikan people under "one god, one aim, one destiny."

We are one people with one culture. While there are many original Afrikan ethnic groups, there is only one Afrikan culture. Others' efforts to fragment us into many incompatible diversities and atomize us into being receptive to the idea that we are, think and act out of many disconnected cultures, or that Afrikan people as a whole are merely an ethnic group instead of many diverse ethnicities within one culture, do not change the fact that we are one. Neither they, nor those among us who speak for them, are qualified to do our thinking for us. However, for some of us, this oneness must still be proven.

Interestingly, Europeans do not have to have this discussion. Hispanics/Latinos do not have to have this discussion. Asians do not have to have this discussion. Arabs do not have to have this discussion. They know they are one people. They know who they are, who their ancestors are, what their traditions are.

Regardless of pretense, Europeans are clear about the fact that every European is a European. *Every* European is genoculturally an active patriot of the european nation. There is no confusion about destiny because every European recognizes (consciously or not) that s/he has a nationbuilding mission.

They are not engaged in meaningless debate over these facts. They are unequivocally sure of their essence and act accordingly without having to think about it or discuss it with others who would dilute their power.

Afrikans, on the other hand, having received the worst of the European, Arab, Asian and, coming, Hispanic assault against our being are not so surefooted in our self-definitions. Our physical, temporal and cultural fragmentation on the Continent and globally, even within our diasporic communities, has caused us to question our unity. Equally detrimental, it has led us to seek out communion with anything other than that which is Afrikan.

As a result of the propaganda spawned by superindividualistic eurocentric minds and the intentional misdefinition of one human race centered around them, Yurugu would now have us define PanAfrikan nationalists as racists.[37] In fact, according to this eureason, any Afrikan who does not want to embrace or bed those who we know to be of the most infamous genocultural aberration in the history of humanity, is deemed racist and childish because of his or her inability to forgive and forget the unforgivable and unforgettable.

It is because of this scientific nonsense that we must continue to prove and emphasize the fact that we, Afrikans, are one people. And, if we are going to rise into that power, we must recognize and act on this fact.

Thoroughness, representativeness and truthfulness in personal evidence is, of course, important for warrior scholars. So, regardless of where on the Continent we search and find evidence of our Afrikan center, we must ever be careful to disentangle what we see and hear in the western intellectualized confusion *now* from what ourstorically prevailed among our people. And we must be extremely careful as we begin to embrace these or any other Afrikan traditions that have come in contact with the contagion we call european culture. For Europeans have spread their "diseased pus" everywhere they did not belong. The European's compromise of all that which once was wholly Afrikan is especially evident among many of those Afrikan traditions which have become politicized and practiced in what is rightfully called New Europe.[38]

The Circle of Centeredness

The *where* of the Afrikan center also requires an explanation that those after a less demanding, more inclusive and open-minded path to the ancestral way might consider limited or closed. Because it is an Afrikan phenomenon, it is not designed for discussion or negotiation outside the sovereign framework of our original, authentic traditions.

We will consider where the Afrikan center is using our Ancestors' most honored shape – the circle. We will diagram it using a concentric model of three spheres (i.e., three, three dimensional circles), one inside the other. This makes sound Afrikan sense. We are a people of the circle. As wholistic visionaries, most of our thinking and creation should follow this eternal dictate.

Moreover, we can look at how the circle applies when we look at how we constructed and managed our spaces. Our Ancestors knew that circles had more area within them than squares of equivalent dimensions. Virtually across the Continent, [39] we see the logical, balanced, protected functionality of the circle. The community reflected this in how it was designed and laid out as circles within circles. For example, each of our compounds were surrounded by (or integrated into) a round wall which kept undesired things and people out. These were the first barrier of external contact. Within each wall there was a relatively open space in which circular houses had been built. These houses provided the innermost privacy, nurturance and protection for the village inhabitants. [40]

Additionally, within the social circles which functioned in these physical circles, we see that everyone was given more than adequate attention and economy in these spaces. Material needs were fulfilled, graded based on knowledge and defensibility. Defense also followed this model. [41] Concentric circles provide the most balanced model of community, regardless of size or resources.

Usually, in the concentric layer or zone concept, circles are used. But we are using "spheres" instead of circles in this analysis because the layers of the Afrikan center must be understood three dimensionally. The center expands or contracts in every direction, including, excluding and responding to all dimensions of the material, mental and spiritual world. These layers are envelopes, integuments, if you will, within which the work and safeguarding of conscious Afrikans occurs.

The Concentric Spheres Model

If you have many farms, you cultivate them all.

Akan Proverb

Using this model, we will identify the Afrikan Center, not as one center, but as a large collection of centers which, together, comprise the Center. We can say that they are a collection of concentrically interconnected communities, or centers, all operating along the path established by one common ancestral mind. In Afrikan spiritual space, they are one, attached to each other at the asilic (cellular) level. They are found in this concentric spherical fashion wherever we have a collection of conscious Afrikans working to be Afrikan. In the alien, anti-Afrikan reality we currently dwell within, though, they may appear to the untrained eye as distinct, multiple centers because they are spatially distanced.

In truth, though, this global connection of seemingly disconnected satellites are not separated by time or space for they find concrete form at the higher levels of Spirit. They only appear so because of how we have been socialized to see this reality and ourselves, when spatially or socially distanced, as fragments. The whole is always there, invisible to eyes without an Afrikan vision.

However, regardless of to what degree we are able to grasp the intangible, permanent nature of the Afrikan center, we have to understand that it is the charge of a select group of self-chosen Afrikan people. It is we who are the eternal carriers of Afrikan truth and practitioners of the Afrikan Way. By our thought, word and deed, we position ourselves within these concentric circles and work together with selfless devotion to keep our Centers safe and functioning.

Our relations are densest at the core, becoming less and less firm as we move toward the outer layers. Beyond the Center's integument, we find ourselves trapped in a deeply mentacidal abyss of self-effacing death, instigated and energized by others. Outside the Center we are but a people struggling for an identity within a world determined to destroy our essence. This twilight zone of the unnatural and unimaginable is a dead, dry, cold place where all hope of being Afrikan is removed and the Afrikan possibility is systematically crushed.

Within our Centers, any vision which psychologically and spiritually dismembers us, materially and physically exploits us and, ultimately, removes us from existence is checked and removed. So, even though the Afrikan Center must always be defined in the context of Spirit, it is reflected and made functional through the thought, word and deed of those who love the Afrikan in themselves and the Universe.

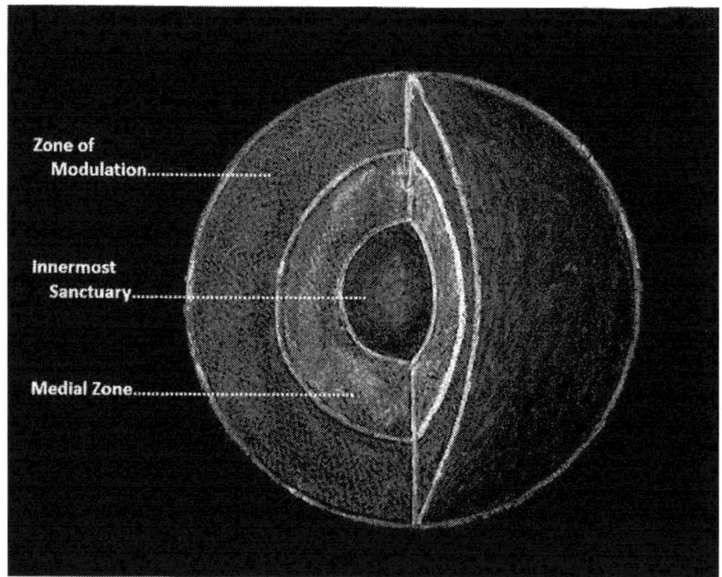

In each of these Afrikan Centers, we have a core, or primary sphere. We have named this space the "Innermost Sanctuary." Here, only the purest traditional Afrikan thought and behavior are found. Moving outward we can see that the "Innermost Sanctuary" is embedded or encased in the "Medial Zone," or secondary sphere. This thick, social sheathing serves as the only substantial buffer against the assault on the practitioners by what has the potential to compromise Afrikan ways.

At the extremities of the centers, we find the most prominent and active frontline. This outer layer we call the "Zone of Modulation," or tertiary sphere. This most peripheral layer is where whatever compromise which may exist within the Centers is most evident. Those who are determined to keep the "Innermost Sanctuary" pure and the filter around it as clean as humanly possible know this exterior sphere is where the vanguard are entrenched. It is the Center's outermost barrier to all which is un- and anti-Afrikan. It is a living barrier to all that is defined as others' insanity.

Ideally, this is the model to which all Afrikan warrior scholars should aspire to build in the interim as ReAfrikanized nationbuilders. While we are in the midst of yurugu's cultural chaos, our time should be consumed with the establishment, development and protection of such Centers of Afrikan power.

Zone of Modulation

Certain popularized aspects of confusion get past the frontline and into this zone. They are carried by Afrikans who claim to be centered but either ignorantly or consciously bring that which is characteristic of others, not us.

This outermost layer is the closest to Yurugu's chaos,[42] being touched by it everywhere there is surface. It is where the greatest assault against the Afrikan Center is waged. And, because the assault against the Afrikan mind has been successfully waged, it has been softened to the point where it is the least intense and abrasive of the cultural and social filters of the two outer layers. Obviously, in a perfect Afrikan world, it would be the strongest and most repellant of that which is not Afrikan. But this is not that world.

The Zone of Modulation is the only point of contact the Afrikan Center has with mentacidal Afrikan minds. It is the physical and psychical space wherein we have the possibility of interacting with the minds of those individuals in the community intent on converting us back to the alien ways they revere. Here is where the most dangerous of the intrusive anti-Afrikan thoughts, words and behavior are modulated and kept from passing on into the two innermost spheres. And, this is why it is the most important frontline of the Afrikan center.

Like the flesh and bone that endures trauma in order to protect vital, sub-epidermal arteries from injury, the Zone of Modulation is the space where the greatest pain is absorbed, isolated and expelled. But it does leave damage. The overlapping scar tissue visibly growing in its outermost regions, in the bodies, minds and spirits of those manning these outposts is a reminder, as are the images of keloid trees, rooted with whips planting psychopathic seeds of insatiable hate into the unbroken backs of enslaved Afrikans, that the war against all that is Afrikan has not yet begun to climax.

Even though they also hold roles at other points in the Center, here are where most of our youngest, brightest and most courageous warrior scholars who spend most of their time engaging alien, enemy encroachments. Here, our most potent, resolute sentries make their stand. Also, this is the portal through which sankofanizing Afrikans, newly discovered of their true selves, enter the Center. As they advance further within the Zone of Modulation, they find themselves members of a living way station. It is a point on our psycho-spiritual underground railroad whose destination is intellectual liberation and not just physical escape from oppression. Here, these relentlessly hunted, worn-down Afrikans begin to truly experience rest as they realize they are free to stop to meditate and study in peace. Here, they begin to accelerate the more intense work of shedding both the external and internalized vestiges of eureason and its pale addictions.

Sadly, so too do we find here, as we found along the underground railroad of a not too distant yesteryear, those who are sinister enough to mask a determined mercenary's errand behind Afrikan faces. Their mission is legend – to more deeply inject the poisons that would enervate our morale, calcify our souls and, eventually, eat away the heart of the inner spheres of our Center. Sometimes doubly confused themselves because of the need to make some new form of Afrikan out of the unalterable old, more than anyone else, it is their malicious intent that keeps the Zone of Modulation in a constant state of flux between relatively secure and insecure states. It is they who constantly remind us that Europeans have never led a successful invasion against Afrikan people, even in a weakened state, without the services of treasonous subversives.

Medial Zone

The Medial Zone is the last buffer before reaching a wholly uncontaminated interior space. In recognizing that when moving from the outer- to the innermost circles that the substance of Afrikan life and consciousness become denser and denser, thereby making the pores through which yurugu's poisons can seep fewer and fewer and smaller and smaller,[43] this layer is not as dense as the sphere that lies safely within it in terms of the incursion of questionable thought and behavior. By the time we reach the core of the Afrikan center, there should be a total absence of compromise. Though, this in no way means there is any meaningful difference in the determination and mentality of the warriors between the three layers.

The Medial Zone is the final filtering mechanism. It is

the last barrier against the tide of others' insanities. And, it serves as the terminal checkpoint for eliminating their useless cultural debris. As the womb is to the fetus, this circle acts as the amniotic fluid of the Afrikan mind, its cushion and protection from external harm.

The Innermost Sanctuary, which sits inside this protective cushion, can be considered the heart of the mental, physical and spiritual space we would equate with the womb. It is not fed by the Medial Zone though. It is protected by it. Spirit, itself, directly nourishes it. The Medial and Modulation Zones are fed in an outward direction from the center of the Innermost Sanctuary. Spirit is both the umbilical cord and the highest uncontaminated, truth and reality that flows through the Innermost Sanctuary into the entirety of the Afrikan mind.[44]

Innermost Sanctuary

For those most serious about our consciousness-raising and protective, nationbuilding undertaking, the answer to the question of "Where is the Afrikan center?," it is here in the Innermost Sanctuary. In this sacred, uncompromised, fully shielded spiritual, mental and physical space lies our true center as a living, endless, unforgetful people on this planet. It is here where we are purest and at our best. For here reside those of us most determined to be wholly Afrikan. We are those who work, determined against all intruders and odds, to earn the greatest respect and garner the most potency from the spirit of our beloved Ancestors.

Here, none but proven Afrikan warrior scholars are welcome. There are no subintegrationists, subassimilationists or subamalgamationists, no negroes or lost souls, no feminists,[45] no homosexualized[46] beings, no Yurugu, here. Here, the line is clearly drawn and held against all odds to the death, because those who are here know that being anything other than Afrikan means death and any within who would attempt to do this are guilty of the heinous crime of treason.

We know that "he who stands on the battle-front does not fear death."[47] For those of us here, as with those of us who formed the highly organized maroon societies, quilombos, guerrilla movements on the Continent and every other Afrikan freedom-fighting collective who recognized and acted on the fact that they were at war, "death before dishonor" is a blood oath freely and solemnly taken by all.

The center of the entirety of the space defined as the Afrikan Center, this Innermost Sanctuary, must be the most vigilantly protected against that which lies outside the greater sphere, and even from the other two spheres encircling it. It must remain inviolable. It cannot be subject to the whim of the corrupted ones enviously seeking to claim it but who are compelled by yurugu's insecurities and imperatives to destroy it. It cannot become the domain of those europhilic traitors who seek nothing less than to corrupt, diffuse and atomize it into nonexistence. Those people, ideas and things which are not Afrikan must never approach our Center.

Those who have now decided to be this ideal type of Afrikan, undifferentiated and undeviating from the way and will of the Ancestors of whom they are spiritually, mentally and physically the culmination, know the responsibility of maintaining and protecting our Innermost Sanctuary from other-oriented innocents, as well as despiritualized, genocidal, insecure predators. They are to be held at no less a standard than those who have already made this commitment and have long acted accordingly. This we all vow to those who have come before and those yet to come.

The core of these concentric spheres must be made sacred because it is here where our classics/holy books are kept and studied in preparation for our full return to power. Certain information, knowledge and wisdom must be retained in the core because of the inability of those in the surrounding zones/circles to keep it close and the greater possibility that they may misinterpret or misuse it or, worse, deliver it to an enemy hiding behind a human disguise.

This discrimination, however, should not be interpreted in the mis-tradition of the "keepers" of Ayi Kwei Armah's "keepers" and "sharers."[48] For the keepers he described who mismanaged our knowledge served the illicit powers that be. Keepers are looking for information to selfishly exploit. "A keeper takes."[49] Sharers are searching for knowledge to convey to the community they serve. Our rightful keepers are also sharers who serve Afrikan power with a clear understanding of the array of negroes and lost souls, as well as Yurugu.

It is only here, in the Innermost Sanctuary, where we are truly Brothers and Sisters, Mamas and Babas. Reciprocity rules. We know we need each other. There is unconditional respect because we understand who we are relative to each other and the Universe. Herein, none exists without family, without love. This is the ancestral vision.

Here, our children are reared, not simply raised,[50] into their power and responsibility as a matter of convention. Mis- and diseducation[51] are distant myths. No one is wasted because our educational institutions are *ours*. Spoilage[52] is inconceivable. Abuse, in any direction, has no place.

Work is done here. We build with direction and in expectation of Afrikan results. We study our Ancestors to identify ourselves. And we design reality with our minds, hearts and bodies to fit that identification. We nationbuild, as one.

Here, in this inner circle, Asafo[53] become Jenoch who age into most honored Elders. In a circle of love and homage, they await transition into guardian Ancestors who rise into a power of which we seem to have lost remembrance.

This is the inner sanctum of the space occupied by our Afrikan Center. This is the home our warrior scholars must build and protect wherever we are if we are to gain liberation and know what to do with it once again achieved.

To avoid confusing the Centers with any part of their

surrounding chaos, we should note that in none of these spheres, even the outermost one, does eureason have a significant foothold. Their relative differentiation and distinction is a measure of the degree to which the members in each zone is accepting or tolerant of eurocentric paraphernalia (ideas, things, people, noneuropean eurocentric advocates, kwk [54]) and ideology being passed off as euroversal [55] or Afrikan. Alienated Afrikans only gain temporary entry through conscious deception. Obviously, blatantly racist eurosupremacists do not penetrate even the outermost layer.

Aspiring warrior scholars also need to be warned about the pseudocenters in our communities whose mission is not to radically empower Afrikan warrior scholars, but to derevolutionize them for Europeans. There are many such organized traps with Afrikan veneers. I prefer to call them "black holes." [56] They can theoretically be defined in the same way that all knowing western science defines that abstractly hypothesized enigma in outer space, which they have never seen and do not have the possibility of knowing about. These "black holes" drape themselves in causes the compassionate warrior naturally gravitates toward.

They are recognizable through their liberalism in political membership and their vehement defense of european ways found among their membership. This cannot be concealed for long from critical thinkers. The problem is disconnecting from them once we become involved. Even for bright minds, it can be difficult to moderate the intensity of the attachments to individuals who knew what they were about but who concealed it from us until we were in too deep to dismiss those pseudo-centers without the pain of disconnection from those whose ideal/image we had learned to love.

Final Thoughts

You cannot have a revolutionary organization where

every possible opinion must be considered valid and worthy of the time it would take to discuss it.[57] At least we cannot have a revolutionary *Afrikan* organization that does so. Any organization of Afrikans who consider themselves revolutionary, who are practicing liberalism, are practicing the art of an ever exponentially fragmenting inclusionism.

In this european dominated reality, there have been extremely few large scale "revolutionary" movements or organizations which were not compromised by the inclusion/infusion of alien ideologies. Confusion is an inherent element in virtually any large scale membership of the oppressed. Their oppressors and indecisiveness insure it. It is not accidental. The exponential fragmentation of truth into any- and everyone's opinion must apply in order to ensure that no real, galvanizing truth about their oppression and their oppressors has solid ground on which to stand unchallenged. Group consciousness is the greatest threat to hegemony.

This is one of Yurugu's more successful disempowering methods. They socialize their victims into a constant state of internal discord. And this dynamic internal chaos prevents them from rectifying the cultural contradictions and interpersonal flaws endemic in the european personality injected into them. This mindless resignation to chaos (because no one is more correct than any other) has oversaturated the very social fiber of Afrikans. Opinions become the rule. And "facts" are selectively sorted to fit ones preferred brand of mentacidal expression.

Subconsciously, for most of us searching for liberation, this ends up being a fight to remove inequality and injustice from our relations with each other without correcting our cultural misorientation. For others, it is the work of bringing self-hatred to a head. In creating more and more difference where it does not exist they, somehow miraculously, become something other than Afrikan. For them, the promotion and endless discussion of the appropriateness of anti-Afrikan difference within the Afrikan community accommodates their ever expanding denial of self. And, in the style of the willful, insatiable masochist, it enables a greater, more direct exploitation by Yurugu.

In any revolutionary Afrikan organization, there must be clear parameters to the limits of acceptable discussion. If there is not, "confusion has a warm place to grow."[58] If there is not a nearly impervious[59] external boundary sheltering all within the conscious community from others' insanities, then there must be layers of boundaries, in the form of series of protective, nurturing concentric spheres. And these must guardedly allow access to more inner circles based on the candidates' demonstrated understanding and practice of the ancestral ideals espoused and most closely approximated in the core.

The outer boundary of each of these spheres within spheres has to be tightly regulated. And the tightness of this regulation should become stricter as one advances closer toward the center. Each boundary represents a threshold of tolerance, or intolerance, if you will, through which no one passes except those who have been tested in the battle of shedding that which they acquired from aliens. The boundaries mark the gradations of that which should have been unlearned and reconceptually relearned in Afrikan terms at those particular points in the Sankofan process of ReAfrikanization. Obviously, those dwelling in the farthest spheres will have shed the least and those in the innermost will have shed the most of that which is not Afrikan.

"Afrikan" Psychologies

To be rewarded or punished by that people is to be created by that people.

Amos N. Wilson

Based on the above discussions, a new, expanded classification system of personality, mentacide and the politics of Afrikan people is in order.   Originally, I limited the range in this description of the variation among us to the broad categories of Afrikans, negroes and lost souls.[60]   Now, there is a definite need for a more refined typology of the categories of people of Afrikan descent for those with the desire to further examine themselves and their character as warrior scholars.   It is called for even the more because each of us is at a different point in the development of this aspiration within ourselves.

Also, unlike before, it has become increasingly more difficult to rationalize calling all Afrikans "Afrikan," especially those consumed by a chronic consciously active condition of self-hatred.   There are those among us who do not deserve the honor of being called Afrikan.   Many warrior scholars have become rightly confused and disturbed over my inclusion of negroes in generic statements about Afrikan people.   I have given this issue a great deal of thought over the last half decade because the recognition that further divisions among Afrikan people, especially initiated internally (even though originating externally[61]), could be seen as serving to extend the time frame for finally resolving the problem of our achieving a sovereign, empowered national unification.

But there comes a time when decisions must be made for the greater warrior scholar good. Confusion among the ranks of those manning the frontlines over who is who leads to defeat after defeat. Confusion feeds delay and then demise among those under systematic assault.

The Qualification

Up to this point, I have used Afrikan as a general category to theoretically and empirically call us all together as a nation of people, asili (genocultural) wise. I have always had reservations about having to include those who have no right whatsoever to inclusion. Those who, with conscious premeditation, have not only relinquished their Afrikan birthright but have also gone so far as to systematically work to take other Afrikans down with them, have made an inclusive Afrikan designation difficult at best.

Yet, as I have already stated, at times, even calling for a well reasoned exclusion of some from the ranks/honor of being Afrikan brings forth virulent accusations that we are adding fuel to the already overwhelming divisiveness perpetrated against us in the war to fragment us into desolate individuals. As Ayi Kwei Armah has so eloquently resolved for us repeatedly:

> That we the black people are one people we know. Destroyers will travel long distances in their minds and out to deny you the truth. We do not argue with them, the fools. Let them presume to instruct us about ourselves. That too is in their nature.[62]

The inclusion of negroes and lost souls as Afrikans still makes "good" sense in this respect. Nonetheless, for warrior scholars actively engaged on the frontline and dealing with people in the community and beyond who actively embrace their mentacidal tendencies, some even venting them against us, this "sense" is becoming less and less suitable.

Also, demographically, in terms of organized numbers, we have not yet given ourselves the authority to remove a segment of the original people from being considered part of our nation, regardless of their level of treason. But, our concern, as warrior scholars, is not with demographics, being politically correct, or any other nonsense which serves to divide us along nationbuilding lines. It would seem that treason would not be the least of these elemental determining factors upon which judgement should be made.

In defining ourselves, our focus naturally and necessarily narrows to align us with those who are courageous enough to man the frontlines, regardless of the odds and/or who does or does not stand beside them. As we do so, it becomes imperative that we speak more concretely and uncompromisingly from the intellectual vantage point of the Asafo, Jenoch and Nsamanfo Nananom of whom we are direct ascendants. [63] I have considered and understand the confusion this may bring. It has been disturbing my subconscious for a while now (like "upper" and "lower" Nile did for many years[64]) but not enough to compel me to divide the range of those for us and those against us within the community into a collection of politically identifiable categories.

This has changed. I have debts, too. Mostly, I owe those who paved the warrior/ReAfrikanized/nationbuilding way. They should never be confused with those who diligently worked to obscure the path or stayed clear of it out of fear and/or repulsion. My discomfort with a general Afrikan designation, and the displeasure over this which has been expressed to me by members of the community over the last few years over placing warrior scholars and the systematically ignorant and notoriously traitorous in the same category by calling them all Afrikan has forced me to do what otherwise would have been a natural progression anyway – clearly distinguish one from the other.

What we are about to present is a positive response to a glaring contradiction to the accepted illogic that, somehow, the violently oppositional politics that fundamentally divide our community can be overlooked for the greater good. The fundamental divide among Afrikans in an anti-Afrikan reality makes nationalist unification impossible, that is unless Afrikan warrior scholars become negroes. For negroes are patently anti-Afrikan.

Consciously pursued studies of these thoroughly oppositional politics (i.e., subassimilationist versus nationbuilding) do not reveal a progressive, equally balanced contribution from each side. Because of their devastating fear, self-hatred and full subsidization by enemies, those among us who are firmly against Afrikan sanity and sovereignty have been historically advantaged. While there may appear to be debate on the surface between europhiliacs and PanAfrikan nationalists, there is a heavy undercurrent that is almost wholly subassimilationist. This begs the question of the possibility of unification in either direction.

Lest we revolutionary nationbuilders forget, there is no real autonomy in the politics of the psychologically disenfranchised. They are merely the inheritors of the politics of the vanquished, a gift from their masters, and that of the revolutionaries (or, better yet, solutionaries[65]), who refuse to commit treason against our Ancestors. So, this civil war within the Afrikan community (where one side is armed with fear and economic-military aid from our enemies and the other side with the courage of our ancestral convictions) is not between sides which see each other as family. At least that is not the negro's perception. They see us as no more than prey meant to be hunted down and killed to win their master's caress.

The negro uses the warrior scholar's gullibility regarding PanAfrikanism as an instrument against us through their mastery of deceit-filled rhetorical ethic.[66] They do not want to be anything Afrikan. And intelligent nationbuilders grant them their wish, however momentarily divisive (in the ourstorical scheme) it may be. Therefore, clarification on who is who politically could prove greatly beneficial to Afrikan sanity. My spiritual, emotional and intellectual senses tell me that this makes perfect sense.

We have already defined negroes as treasonous, duplicitous minions of lesser gods, as clowns, sellouts, willing overseers and drivers, consciously other-oriented, self-hating eunuchs and disease-lovin' afrophobes. [67] They have thoroughly earned a lower case "n." As those dead, willfully turned from Afrikan spirit, who look like us but who model treason, who still walk in our midst consciously defiling our heritage and possibilities, their names should only be called in disgust. To be clear, negroes are in league with Europeans and, in many instances, are leading them against us. negroes do not negotiate with warriors, except on behalf of their masters, and then only to stall us so that their masters can better plan against our unification.

> These are Blacks who obscure or deny the reality of racial oppression, for personal monetary rewards or in anticipation of white affection, and who care little or nothing about the survival and progress of other members of their own racial group....[These individuals] maintain, rather than challenge, the racial order in America, ultimately serving that country's pursuit and practice of white racial sovereignty and domination.[68]

Among a people in flight from self there will be much confusion. An insatiable self-hatred will prevail as long as they run. It will manifest itself in destructive ways which systematically/directly benefit those they are running toward. And it will, at the same time, work against them. The logic of this flight will in no way carry an understanding of the true reasoning for their flight. It is within and against themselves and, therefore, hidden from them.

Those Afrikans with a loathing self-hatred, running toward whiteness at breakneck speed while cursing the blackness they cannot outdistance, will attribute all that is good and worthy in the Universe and their lives to the magic of european civilization. The worse will be credited to our origins. In flight from any and everything Afrikan, even those aspects condoned by Yurugu, until these master appropriators publicly claim them as their own, negroes are trying to create a world where Europeans can live in peace with their crimes against the Universe and forever walk safely among those they have uprooted and destroyed. negroes want to be the first picked among those chosen to be walked among.

Their treason is unforgettable and, in most cases, unforgivable.[69] And we must act accordingly. An elder in our community here has given us a shining example of what our response to them should be whenever and wherever we have gathered in solemn communion with our Ancestors. While pouring libation for us, he also takes a moment to pour for them. But, instead of pouring their libation in the ground of our sacred space as he does for us, he goes outside to spit that portion of the liquid reserved for them on the dead concrete to welcome them away. They must be dismissed and distanced as we do any other contagion.

Hopefully, the evolving typology presented here will facilitate a more sensible labeling. It should allow Afrikans, who know they are Afrikan in revolutionary thought, revolutionary word and revolutionary deed, to locate themselves in a unique, worthy and untainted spiritual and intellectual classification.

Nonetheless, those of us who have traveled a long and hard road to become Afrikan have to realize that there are transitional zones within our movement from an ignorant enemy self, addicted to insanity, to being the living embodiment of our warrior Ancestors. We know that any such scientific portrayal of differences in mentality among a given people must take this into account.

Those moving toward their Afrikan selves travel along a continuum. So, even before beginning, we can expect that this typology will address some form of mentality spectrum. Still, obviously, there will/must be clearly mutually exclusive segments based on the thoughts, words and deeds of the individuals involved.

A Typology of People of Afrikan Ascent[70]

Afrikan Warrior Scholars – This group of dedicated, uncompromising frontline Elders, Jenoch and Asafo are staunch revolutionaries who are fighting for the liberation of Afrikan people. We recognize that we are our Ancestors. Further, we are clearly conscious, so we have no reason to question our being at war for the remembrance, elevation, empowerment and sovereign liberation of Afrikan people. These indefatigable warriors thrive on a strict intellectual diet of proven, liberating ideologies, methodologies and exercises. Always in a state of preparedness, always ready for any exigency, our work is conditioned by the situation. Nonetheless, whatever the situation may be, first and foremost, we turn to the lessons left us by our Ancestors for operational instruction for any given exigency. Our vision of a whole Afrikan people determines the strategies and tactics which will consistently, correctly guide us along the Afrikan Way in any given circumstance, whatever the conditions, whoever the enemy, however few or many our numbers. We are the workers in our Centers.

Nationalist Intellectualizers – Nationalist intellectualizers are armchair "revolutionaries," bereft of consequential action, who misdefine debate as the most fruitful way of engaging our rhetorically experienced enemy. They are still living in the fantasy that Europeans can be talked out of their racism and that racism is a "human" fluke of which the european manifestation is said to be but one expression and, in the scheme of things, no better or worse than any others. These masters of meaningless debate are intellectually distanced from the "masses," except to the extent of using them as fodder in their political efforts to force others to embrace them in a conversation in which, regardless of the radical nature of their statement, they hope will lead to their validation by them. No matter their pronouncements, they are constantly in search of european allies. These individuals, and all types following this category, are european user-friendly.

<u>Humanist Reactors</u> – Deracialized/acultural activists, agitators and anarchists (often self-proclaimed, proselytizing marxist and other "we're all human," "pain is pain"[71] socialists) fit into this category. Also included in this motley crew are feminists, homosexualized "warriors"[72] and their advocates, as well as spiritualists who see themselves as being above race and politics, at least where nonAfrikans are concerned.[73] Here also lie some members of the old guard who have chosen to rest on the laurels of their former revolutionary stands. These erstwhile and/or impotent "revolutionaries" have lost their credibility as a dynamic force and make every effort to convince themselves, and have others believe, that their changeability is for our betterment. (Interestingly, they are most opposed to those coming behind them who have chosen to pick up their fallen spears because of what it may reveal about limits of their vision and/or their ineptitude.) But, in truth, they do no more than make public spectacles of themselves by expressing their forgiveness[74] of and infusing a nonexistent humanity into Yurugu in order to stay in the public eye, be validated by the powers that be and, from their old enemies/new masters, gain a larger share of the trinkets which were once reserved exclusively for the career negroes they once fiercely condemned in order to create a more visible space for themselves on the "minority" stage. "To be rewarded or punished by that people is to be created by that people."[75]

<u>Lost Souls</u> – These individuals bend over backwards to avoid

any genocultural issues/issues of race whose analysis may upset Europeans or other groups they consider the diviners of this reality. They are masterful evaders of conflict with empowered agents of eurosupremacy. As such, they are particularly skilled at hiding from any possible "fallout" from being in proximity to serious warrior scholars. Often, these shadowy "runners" are veterans at studied nonobservance,[76] i.e., skilled pretenders at "not seeing" the obvious. They still wear the mask.

<u>Rejecters</u> – Slightly more political than lost souls, rejecters are those individuals who consciously evade any Afrikan who even slightly appears to be controversial or revolutionary. Though, unlike lost souls, they may engage in "serious" discussion of racial issues, it is always from the perspective of the racial status quo. They are always their job, degree, position, kwk. first, and African (american) second, third, fourth, fifth or, better yet, in their minds last, if at all. Rejecters seek shelter in predominantly european, arab or asian environments (businesses, communities, religious organizations and faiths, beds, kwk.)

<u>Sympathetic (Apologetic) Proselytizers</u> – Sympathetic proselytizers want to save us. They want to assist us out of our misguided ways into safer, more submissive, roles. They want to assist us redirect our energy toward welcoming yurugu's society's "good" into our hearts, while dissipating whatever "anger issues" we have with apologies rationalizing as unavoidable yurugu's "bygone" behavior (if not trying to convince us that it was for our good). They believe they are releasing us from unnecessary troubles by reeling us back into the seductive, narcotized comfort mentacide brings them. In their minds, what they do is for our benefit and protection. They believe we are just pigheadedly confused. And they consider themselves on a mission of protecting us from ourselves. Their love is genuine, but exercised out of

ourstorical, political ignorance and a historically reasonable fear for what may happen to us for confronting evil. They recognize their blackness, but their "loyalty" is based more on a belief in its permanence than its significance. Such individuals are content to live with whatever change the negro misleadership articulates for them.

<u>Apathetic Proselytizers</u> – This group of other-directed individuals believe they can demean conscious Afrikans into submission to the european way. Like sympathetic (apologetic) proselytizers, they work to change our politics and cultural direction. But they do so for selfish reasons. They fear Afrikan warrior scholars because of what we may mean for them relative to white backlash or others' perceptions of them by others because of a relation to us, which cannot be altered without enormous legal and/or personal difficulty. Their fear is for self, not based on a concern for us. Most of them just want to bring us down to their level so that they can feel elevated above us. Most are keenly aware that our presence exposes their mentacide.

<u>Hateful Eunuchs</u> – Hateful eunuchs hold an intense, perpetual self-hating rage against their genocultural self and other Afrikans. The expression of this self-hatred is especially reserved for those fighting for the reascension of Afrikan power. However, they do so without power or influence and live in fear of retaliation by Afrikans they may attempt to vent their frustrations against. They are ever tortured by their own foolishness and commit acts of powerlessness in an effort to conceal their self-hatred from themselves.

<u>Passive (apolitical) negroes</u> – Though they clearly know who they are striking out against, these europhilic mercenaries are the premier underminers of conscious Afrikans and Afrikan efforts, but only because there are many more of them than the active, calculating kind. Nonetheless, even when they try, they

are unsystematic and erratic in their operations against us.   And this is because they are not politically astute enough to understand why they want to do what they try to do against us. And, even when they do understand, they only accidentally make the connection between our people's condition and their role as agents of Afrikan subjugation.   Their validation and defense by Yurugu and their resultant arrogance lead them to mistakenly hold little fear of Afrikan warrior scholars.

<u>Active (calculating) negroes</u> – These negroes systematically and consistently work to undermine conscious Afrikans and our efforts.   They take special pride in subverting and weakening us.   They are not confused as to why they do what they do against us and for whom it is done.   They are consciously, intentionally deceitful.   And, because they are bolder than their passive counterparts, they are more aware of our knowledge of them and keenly cognizant of their fears of us.   Their primary mission is to utterly destroy or, at least, reduce to the appearance of a babbling lunacy, any Afrikan who would dare to stand and attempt to wage mental, physical and/or spiritual war against Europeans, or any others for whom they have been enlisted as praetorian watchdogs.   It is negroes who, on bended knee in the heat of their destruction, pitifully cry out to their tormentors from the abyss of powerlessness, "Can't we all just get along?"   And, in their longings to be crowned saviors in our destroyers' eyes, they beseech them so, again and again and again.   These devout traitors comprise the most dangerous battalion in the internally coordinated assault against Afrikan people.   They are consciously subintegrationist, subassimilationist and subamalgamationist.   And their politico-economically[77] dictated nepotism and pathways to the european-validated reigns of influence are highly organized, tightly regulated and well subsidized by their european benefactors.

<u>Nonblacks</u> – The most self-hating of all, nonblacks have

brainwashed themselves (or willed others to brainwash them) to the point where they truly believe that they are "not Black." These are the active, visible deserters. They admit to no Afrikan being (unless highly profitable). A full denial of any Afrikan self characterizes the vast majority of them. Most pride-filled bi- and multi-racial individuals fall into this category of new Europeans. Interestingly, negroes and lost souls spend an enormous amount of energy trying to claim them and/or convince them of their "blackness" in order to get some racial credit for their privilege and/or notoriety.

<u>Crossovers/Passers</u> – Invisibility is actually attained in this group of crossover aspirants composed of those who are phenotypically able to lose themselves in whiteness. They closely, if not completely resemble Yurugu physically. These are the most active and successful deserters of the Afrikan race.[78] Yet, in most cases they are oblivious to their treason because their appearance makes it easy for them to pass for the melaninless being they so desire to be or truly feel they are. They experience no such contradictory feelings because they *see* no biological connection between themselves and Afrikan people. Having been born with, or cosmetically or surgically altered to have "the bluest eyes," they are the invisible deserters, slipping completely through the cracks of Afrikanity[79] into whiteness.

Another Useful Typology

Another useful typology is found in Kwame Agyei Akoto's *Nationbuilding*.[80] He lists three identities most often assumed by Afrikans in response to white racism.[81] From the most defeatist to the most progressively optimistic, they are named "denial and avoidance," "defensive accommodation" and "active resistance."

1)   The truly vanquished and those who believe in the sacredness of white supremacy languish in a state of "denial and avoidance".   These individuals

a.   deny any Afrikan origin or connection (except that which is pushed by their overlords and serves defensive purposes against them),

b.   insist on being amalgamated into what they deem a superior physical and mental type,

c.   single-mindedly pursue their rapid and complete assimilation of the european way and,

d.   as an expected reward for the services they render their masters, feel they deserve nothing less than a full pardon for being Afrikan and an unconditional subassimilation into european culture and society.

These individuals methodically search for ways to distance themselves from everything Afrikan, especially Afrikans who are not working with them toward white acceptance.   We can easily guesstimate that sixty percent or more of all Afrikans fall into this category.

2)   "Defensive accommodation" is purely reactionary. Reaction, in an oppressive social context, should be distinguished from action in that an action utilizes (is motivated by) foresight and insight (preparedness and expectation through study of the assailant's historical pattern of thought and behavior, as well as common, self-preserving Afrikan sense).   A reaction, on the other hand, is an unplanned response to what should be expected but to which the respondent remains unaware and unprepared because he or she is unable (or unwilling) to connect the act with the normal thought and behavior of the source.   He or she is unable to see or, more likely for Afrikans relative to Europeans, believe that such incidents could occur repeatedly.

Unlike reaction, action is not a response based on being surprised by a known assailant.   It is aggressively preemptive or, if the offense is unpredictable by any means, as in terrorism, cautious and guarded. Actions are planned. Reactions are not.

This reactionary thought and behavior tend to be expressed in various revealing ways. Such individuals offer a self-serving defense of their progressive subassimilation into western society using the excuse of being the chosen agents of some coming raceless humanism by changing the Europeans and their "system" from inside out. They have moved beyond belief in accepting that the ultimate form of validation comes from Europeans and european institutions. To this they have dedicated and voluntarily given their lives.

Even so, in order to conceal their mentacide and the sacredness they attribute to their motives, they conspicuously decorate themselves and their homes in appropriate amounts of Afrikan attire and paraphernalia. Their diet mirrors the latest health findings of our most conscientious, dedicated and scientific homeopaths, naturopaths and nutritionists. And, you can be sure that they will be present and accounted for at whatever conferences, events and other activities where committed Afrikans should be in attendance. They are the kind of chameleons whose character we cannot count on in war.

Possibly most alarming, they have read and shelved many of the analytically correct books pertaining to ourstory. This is all the more troubling because any fearless, open, intelligent study and comprehension of truly Afrikan centered material should not logically lead them in a direction politically opposing us or, rather, themselves. Those who have studied the master Jenoch, with an Afrikan mind, tend not to use them as a shield to conceal, or somehow validate as culturally eclectic, their europeanization.

Obviously, for the genoculturally sighted, these "learned" shadows of Yurugu have no more than a superficial, utilitarian relationship with Afrikan imagery and being. Feigned displays of Afrikanity are only defensive maneuvers calculated to defend them against both the European's contempt and the Afrikan warrior's knowing gaze.

These closet europhiliacs, so painfully trapped in Afrikan skin, most closely resemble what would be the modern, materially pampered version of W.E.B. DuBois' Afrikans who feel they have been unfairly caught behind a suffocating veil of blackness. They flounder about in uncertain states of cognitive dissonance, [82] caught or, rather, torn between an Afrikan unconsciousness and a more desired eurocentric identity. By Dubois' own description,

> It is a peculiar sensation, this double-consciousness, the sense of always looking at one's self through the eyes of others, of measuring one's soul by the tape of a world that looks on in amused contempt and pity. One ever feels his twoness – an American, a Negro; two souls, two thoughts, two unreconciled strivings; two warring ideals in one dark body, whose dogged strength alone keeps it from being torn asunder.[83]

Consciousness of their "dark body" does little to curb their desire for acceptance by Europeans. They see their Afrikan shell as a prison deserving of their hatred only. At the same time, they feel compelled to publicly declare a self-love for fear of being exposed for their self-hatred.

Racial captivity is their lot. In their deranged interpretation of self and this reality, their "plight" is a fate worse than death. They remain mortified, insulted by their sable existence, unable to be the European of their dreams, entrapped in an oppressive, racialized purgatory.

It is here where we find the homosexualized Afrikans who are advertising themselves as "centered." Other self-alienated beings occupying this space, also claiming an Afrikan center, are those who are married to Europeans or otherwise ideologically sleeping with the enemy. Sadly, many "Afrikan centered" spiritualists and a good portion of "Afrikan centered" schools are also riding the wave of Yurugu's delusional colorless, genderless new humanity.[84] It is an ignoble space shared by a motley crew hopelessly in denial of their self-hatred.

Probably thirty percent of Afrikans fit into this category of dedicated fencewalkers. Still, again and again in Afrikan garb, they rise from european beds, lifestyles and mentalities.

3) "Active resistance" is the most productive response for warrior scholars. It describes the thought and behavior of those who expend their energy doing the difficult and immediately thankless work of

      a. solidly reconnecting us to the knowledge and wisdom of our Ancestors,

      b. practicing our traditions without modification (Active resisters do this using an informed, critical understanding of what to keep and toughen and what to ignore and discard based on our historical and ourstorical understanding of what has and has not worked for us over our time on this planet) and

      c. building strong, empowered, enduring institutions that reaffirm the Afrikan Way in such a manner that it can no longer be assaulted by internal or external enemy forces.

Akoto fully recognizes that there is a range in the purity of the politics of those who actively resist the european cultural hegemony and physical domination of Afrikan people. And it begins at the farthest point where those who seek european validation in any form are at their worst and extends itself in progressive Sankofan fashion to the most completely reAfrikanized warrior scholars. However, he makes it clear that it is only at the most conscious, centered end of this spectrum where our thinking soldiers are capable of seeing and acting upon the extraordinary mission of uncompromisingly building one sovereign Afrikan nation.

> Our task is not a minor one. Our task is nationbuilding,
> and the guiding directive must be to build the nation.
> The vision is one of a truly self sufficient Afrikan nation
> peopled by families and individuals bound to a code of

ethics and committed to advancing the cultural heritage
of our people.   Our vision must remain clear, and not be
clouded by seemingly interminable problems and crisis.
We must approach our vision with an informed faith, not
a blind faith.   That faith must be one that is informed by
a critical knowledge of our history, our cultural reality and
the current world conditions.   It must be a faith borne of
unqualified confidence of the justice of our efforts, our
ability to successfully hurdle any obstacle, and in the
knowledge that the souls of all those who struggled before
us will aid us and cover our backs.[85]

This indefatigable group probably comprises
somewhere around ten percent of the Afrikan nation, although
only about five percent are truly, fully committed and actively
involved in our liberation movement.   The other five percent
are mostly closet, armchair or paper "revolutionaries," aware
individuals floating in and out of active Afrikan consciousness.

It is because of these differences in character and
consciousness among Afrikan people that we must again be
clear about just who are this book's intended readers.   When a
people are at war for the survival of their sanity, any
compromise, indecision or disloyalty becomes liabilities which
automatically benefit those who seek to destroy them.   On this
there can be no confusion.

There is no grey area in war.   There is no space for
wishy washy soldiers or those who have misdefined soldiery for
an exercise in subassimilation, i.e., those who make loud
revolutionary noises only so that the enemy will let them in to
silence their tirades.

The "New" Afrikan

[N]ationbuilding can occur only in the context of traditional Afrikan culture and cosmology....less the distortions born of non-Afrikan encroachment and degradation....Nationbuilding must be understood as a process of reconnection and continuity. Nationbuilding does not start with a blank slate. Nationbuilding is not about creating a 'new' man or a 'new' cultural reality using eclectic cultural and ideological borrowings from a panoramic variety of cultural formations and philosophies. For us, nationbuilding is an intergenerational process of progressive but intense denuding ourselves of multi-generational layers of alien values and thinking, and the progressive adoption and immersion of ourselves in the culture and the work of rebuilding.

Kwame Agyei and Akua Nson Akoto

ReAfrikanization requires that we return to our original being. It is the process by which we remake ourselves into our authentic Afrikan form in thought, word and deed. And, this must occur while we are fully cognizant of both our people's captivity in this alien, anti-Afrikan reality and our need to remain models of Afrikanity under these trying conditions.

Although, to some, it may sound like we are trying to discover something new, ReAfrikanizing Afrikans are simply uncovering that which already exists in us. We have remained deceived through a mentacidal socialization in the hands of enemies and the mercenary workforce they have anchored among us. It is because of this that the Afrikan within has remained dormant. Just as any good educator knows that the work lies in opening the students' eyes to their own genius, who we are is already within us awaiting our awakening.

A number in the so-called revolutionary mix, however, have misdefined ReAfrikanization as an effort to create a newly defined Afrikan, one more in line with an ideology that portrays Afrikans as little more than Europeans with melanin.[86] They have muddled and misdefined the meaning of New Afrikan in the same way as they have created and hidden behind a compromised definition of Afrikan Centered.

Confused over our origin and evolution as an intelligent civilization, these cultural saboteurs define european faults (racism, sexism, ageism, warmongering, kwk) as everyone's tradition and way. Even worse, they visualize the ReAfrikanized Afrikan in the image of a healed, humanized European. Accordingly, this "new" Afrikan is defined quite differently from the "old" Afrikan, for his creators operate on the premise that the Maafan [87] process (genetic rape, dehumanization, deculturalization, destruction of homeland and sense of nationalism, kwk) which severely corrupted tradition-grounded, untainted Afrikans is irreversible. They depict this broken, transformed caricature of our Ancestors as something from which we can no longer divest ourselves. Some, even like those they disparagingly critique as negroes, see this as a positive. This newly deformed being is defined as the outcome of a natural socio-cultural human evolution, as progress away from primitivity, barbarity, backwardness and tradition.

In truth, though, this "new" Afrikan is the self-rationalization of vanquished Afrikans trying to claim a revolutionary standing. Publicly, loudly, persistently, they promote themselves in the image of something other than their subintegrative and subassimilative selves. Their aspirations do not take them beyond this insanity.   In reality, their vision is of such grandeur within this insanity as to literally be impossible. It is a dream of revolutionaries seeking asylum among their oppressors by espousing an impossible but lofty revolutionary goal which distracts from their true self-rationalizing intent.

For many who use it, "new" Afrikan is a designation for those who want the honor of being Afrikan without giving up their european ways.   Claiming this "new," blended, deculturalized identity for themselves allows the rationalization of incorporating what is not Afrikan (such as feminism and homosexuality) into their being as normal and acceptable. They have become something new (an automatic positive in their eyes) and different (another out of context positive).

Their loss of true identity is concealed behind some concocted fabrication of a new, all-inclusive, genderless, oppressionless [88] humanity (auto-correcting of persistent european flaws) that is in an almost psychotic denial of its self-evident europeanization in blackface.   Even as a sane ideal, this "new" human is an impossibility within the bounds of european culture.   There can be no Afrikan in the european mind.   In these cases, the "new" Afrikan is no more than an initiated negro in mudcloth, an ex-Afrikan who is part of "everything" but without substance.   Any intelligent Afrikan should know that "one does not use oneself as an ingredient in a medicine requiring that the ingredients be pulverized."[89]

Obviously, despite these apologetic attempts to make our physical and cultural rape appear benign, there are no "new" Afrikans.   We are our Ancestors.   Under any assault we are still the oldest of humanity.   If we are to use the term "New Afrikan," then it must be reconceptualized to fit this understanding.   It must be used as a rallying cry calling us to war against becoming something other than what we have always been and always will be.

Reconceptualized thusly, the "New Afrikan" is one who is revolutionary enough to be ancestral in an un- and anti-Afrikan time and place.   "New Afrikans," then, correctly defined, are those of us who have formed the new vanguard of the timeless, functional, progressive, dynamic Afrikan Way. These are newly awakened Afrikans, not newly miscreated ones.

True ReAfrikanization

Afrikans in search of a true ReAfrikanization do not seek a partial or compromised return to our Way. We seek an unqualified return to the nurturing spirit, consciousness, genius and humanity of our Ancestors. This is the path we choose to follow, no matter how difficult or impossible it may seem to those whose vision has been limited by a conditioned inability to recognize that nothing is impossible for the Afrikan genius.

Some, lost to the suffocating, identity-less oblivion of vanquishment, hold their hands over their ears and scream to the heavens that we are grasping at impossibilities. But we know that the vision of a victorious people is never small. We know that there are no limits to the Afrikan genius. We know the stars.[90]

Again, as the prefix "re" implies, ReAfrikanization is a return home in thought, word and deed. It is the re-becoming of what we already are but which we have lost sight of due to circumstances beyond our control and often memory. Through the process of ReAfrikanization, we rise above those hateful forces set in motion which compel us to voluntarily deny ourselves. As Kwame Agyei and Akua Nson Akoto inform us, "ReAfrikanization is the rediscovery, redefinition and revitalization of the Afrikan reality and way of being."[91]

ReAfrikanization, then, occurs within the framework of Sankofa. Our Sankofa occurs when remembrance is facilitated through looking back to our traditions *only* and all they entail in order to define ourselves and our actions in the here and now. Without this we remain unable to gather within that spectacular effort needed to create, out of the morass of chaos, a future more fitting to who we are as a people. It is the actualization of our return to "our center of gravity, our cultural and spiritual mother, our beating heart."[92]   For, in no other way can we become who we are, except through spiritually and mentally becoming our Ancestors.

Since part of the ReAfrikanization process is reclaiming our native tongue, we should also reintroduce the Akan term *Odwira*[93] here. Odwira simply means "purification," and is a most appropriate descriptive for the process of ReAfrikanization. For ReAfrikanization is a full cleansing of the soul, mind and body. It is a conscious effort to remove what does not belong and bring back what was wrongly displaced. Through ReAfrikanization balance is restored through a burning away of the useless, retarding dross (european cultural domination) to expose the timeless gold (Afrikan spirit/culture).

ReAfrikanization is the method whereby we submerge ourselves into and submit our consciousness to the will and way of those who initiated and lived our personal and genocultural lineage. It is a psychological return to the source of the spiritual and physical truth of who we are. It is to again become Afrikan.

ReAfrikanization occurs when we take what we are learning through this submersion and submission and begin to apply it to ourselves in an effort to change ourselves, from that which we have been forced to imitate and exaggerate, into our true selves, into our Ancestors. It is a process wrought with difficulty and hardship because our mentacide is extensively rooted in eureason. And, eureason, being an extension and defense mechanism of european people, logically binds everything we mentacidally believed with a reality, which though alien and anti-Afrikan, is accepted as logical, rational and desirable. The anti-Afrikan crusade coming from without and within assaults us from every possible angle and in virtually every thought to the point where it is ofttimes overwhelming. But, once we know we are Afrikan, once we know we are not European, nothing eureason brings can stop us from being who we are.

ReAfrikanization is how we rise into our Afrikan selves. Through it, we begin the conscious, collective process of changing our environment to match our growing awareness of how an Afrikan world would and should feel for us in overcoming this harsh, despiritualized time and place. As we think as the Afrikans we are, we become the Afrikans we have always been.

ReAfrikanization is a personal transformation. It is a return to self. We actually become our Ancestors. And, with time, and the elevation of significant numbers of Afrikans into consciousness, it becomes a communal and, then, global national transformation.

Afrikans trying to help invent a "new" world wherein they can finally feel human without "the curse" of having to be Afrikan, do so pretending that this reality is not dominated by, and wholly rooted in, european imperatives. These "out with the old, in with the new" individuals are operating under the delusional assumption that they are the vanguards of a new deculturalized humanity. Frightened of their Afrikan selves, these severely psychologically damaged outpatients of yurugu's asylum are claiming that they are even breaking away from the very idea of tradition.

Forgetting that "a slave's wisdom is in his master's head,"[94] some are even claiming to have no traditions, except those which they now manufacture for themselves out of what they conveniently and reactively select of the eurocentrically interpreted past and present realities. From deep within the Afrikan nation, this rootless, superindividualistic movement has shown itself to possess a growing schizophrenic ignorance of just how tradition is created and what it is designed to do. They have mistakenly located the source of their vanquishment and oppression in the failure of our tradition, and not with yurugu's evil genius. No people aspiring to power, or who have attained power, dismiss their truth and lineage and remain powerful.

For serious nationbuilders who recognize the importance of tradition to accurately defining oneself, the very thought of forgetting oneself is laughable because *no* individual functions without a tradition. No group of individuals can start a society from nothing because someone taught them how to think and live. And, in that teaching, the tradition of the instructor is thereby subconsciously transferred.

This should be obvious. No society is started by newborns. And socialization, which is no more or less than a life's instruction in the traditions which evolved out of the original or implanted cultural way of that people, begins at first contact with physical reality.

No matter how we look at it, every people follows a tradition. This is no less so for those vanquished Afrikans confused enough to pretend that they do not follow their enemy's tradition. Arguments against the inextricable relevance of tradition are no defense against this ourstorical and historical truth. In the oppositional european cultural context, where everything must be contrasted and all contrasts made hierarchical,[95] if truly being Afrikan is not what we want, then we are fighting for further subintegration, further subassimilation, further subamalgamation, in other words, for a kinder, more benign genocide.

Every people *is* a tradition. No people is separable from their tradition unless they are no longer that people.

To counter this mentacidal expression of detached uniqueness/superiority, as well as any other initiative which leads us to question the need and value of walking in a traditional Afrikan Way, we must know that tradition reflects a core evolving, adaptive property. It is a real, dynamic expression of culture. It is not stagnant, stuck in some archaic, outdated, outmoded, primitive, backward, useless, dysfunctional past totally out of sync with any contemporary, functioning, competitive reality. For tradition is no more or less than all of the intellectual, mechanical and metaphysical technology which naturally maintains a people as they have come to see themselves in this universe. It is the result of untold generations consciously working together to correct their errors and perfect those corrections. Tradition is the culmination of all that has been tried and proven true through the experience of a people. It defines that people's worth and existence. Without tradition a people cease to exist. "To forget is to terminate."[96]

For these reasons and more, we must get over the idea that *our* traditions, in and of themselves, but especially relative to the european's, are liabilities that are bad, dysfunctional or useless. "That which one comes upon is nothing to compare to what one has always had."[97] We must stop allowing others to convince us that most traditions do not make sense, and do not have to make sense, and therefore can be discarded at will because they served people "way back then" when conditions, knowledge and expectations are said to have been based on ludicrous superstition, bogus mythology and an absence of rational scientific thinking. It is in response to this nonsense that, increasingly, confused Afrikans allow themselves to conclude that there is no such thing as culture, except that which they, at this moment, bring into existence.

Otherwise, we are accepting the validity of another's traditions while dismissing the relevance of ours in knowing self and empowering the Afrikan nation. This desire to ignorantly live in peace with Yurugu through ourstorical, genocultural invisibility seems a sound terminal strategy for many. Knowing self and empowering Afrikan people are not worthwhile issues for misoriented, subassimilation-seeking individualists.

Tradition is unquestionably timeless. It does not change its essence. Its imperatives to not age. It only modifies its expression (customs), given environmental (social and physical) change.

So, by definition, Afrikan culture is adaptive. "It is malleable. It changes under the pressure of changing circumstances, but it changes in order to remain the same."[98]

When we take a good, long look at our culture as a functional expression of our people over the duration of our existence, we can see that, regardless of its adaptations, its essence, its critical content, the content which defines us as Afrikan people, remains unchanged.

Looking at our Way through an uncompromised, healthy Afrikan centered perspective allows us to reflect on and embrace the process of creative cultural and social engineering that began molding our traditions many thousands of generations ago. This process began when Afrikans began. It began with us and we began with it. And because we share life and truth with it, it is still there, waiting on our return and reclamation.

The logic behind Afrikan traditions has not changed with the passage of time because it still makes sense for us. And that will never change because we will always be Afrikan. Our collective personality custom designed those traditions to fit us. And they, in turn, reinforced us.

In the process, the cultural foundation came into a life of its own, a life that has lasted throughout all our generations. It lives as an eternal entity, a beacon to our identity, expressing itself through us whose ancestors thought it into existence to serve and protect us. It is constant with us until we are no more, and we will always be.

The values and beliefs it prescribes for its adherents determine the form our traditions take in whatever environment and state we find ourselves, for they can but model its essence. And we should note that the values and beliefs that come out of this cultural foundation are inseparable from it. Therefore, they do not change either.

If anything changes it is the people who are the culture's heirs. And, when people change, what they believe to be and honor as their traditions, change accordingly. But, as we can see here, in this time and place, it is not really the traditions that change. People in doubt and fear, and/or who are in love with individualistic survival and greed, move away and lose sight of what their ancestors' gave them. It is they who substitute others' traditions for their own in defiant acts of cutting, suicidal self-hatred.

When referring to our culture, we say "traditional" only to distinguish it from that anti-Afrikan culture found today in so many Afrikan communities globally. Most of what we currently see in our communities bears witness to successful invasion. For, what we see is not wholly us. It is the product of original Afrikan culture being infected and supplanted by european culture.

Warrior scholars say "traditional" because the confused among us see this newly miscreated cultural order as representing a modernized, but still genuine, Afrikan culture. And we know that it is not. If this supplantation were to become complete, what would exist would no longer be Afrikan culture. It would be european culture, no matter the race of the practitioners.

Therefore, to save us from this confusion, we will use the word "traditional" as our descriptive adjective when speaking of untainted Afrikan culture. And, again, we should always remember that Afrikan culture, in its pure form does not change with time. Afrikan culture is Afrikan culture whether then or now. Modernity, or modernization, does not change it into something else. The trappings alien invaders force it into do not alter its existence. Its asili, its spiritual core, remains constant, being neither old nor new. Time is irrelevant. It is always as it is.

So, we are only using the word "traditional" here to identify it in its *original* form. This "traditional" is not subject to the vagaries of european time. It is itself whether now or at any other point in "time" we study it. We must be clear on this definition because of the massive amount of misinformation circulating about what is wrong with traditional, noneurocentric interpretations of reality and the advantages negroes and lost souls experience when being blended into the insanity we know as american (i.e., european) culture.

Actually, there is nothing wrong with the word traditional itself. A problem arises only when we misguidedly, comparatively misdefine it for ourselves as an ourstorically, culturally conservative people relative to what we have been led to believe is the superior, contemporary or modern culture(s) of others. This intellectual acquiescence reduces us to dealing in eureason, thinking against our own interests and in favor of those of Europeans. And the worst part of us allowing ourselves to think in this way is that it leaves us unable to see that Europeans are what they have always been. They have not changed. "The stump that stays in a river for a hundred years does not become a crocodile."[99]

Unlike so many of us, they have never stopped practicing their most ancient and sacred traditions. They have simply dressed them up in their glitter and our genius, mentacidally twisted and embroiled in the glorification of this glitter,[100] to conceal their true nature and intent from us.

Traditions

Therefore, if we are to be Afrikan warrior scholars, internalizing and expressing every intent of the concept, if we are going to put forth the extraordinary time and energy necessary to ReAfrikanize ourselves, to again nationbuild, we must go back into our ancestral spirit to retrieve and, then, consciously participate in our Way. We must also seriously study the working traditions it engendered and answer the questions of why these particular thoughts and behaviors were best suited for maintaining a dynamic Afrikan sanity. We have to accept and trust our ancestors' wisdom. And we must not allow a europeanized sense of time to alter our practice of the traditions our Ancestors mastered.

If we are to truly be Afrikan, and not some mentacidal, artificial version of it subsisting under european cultural domination, we cannot commit treason against our Ancestors'

Way.   For to commit treason against them is to betray ourselves.   We are our Ancestors.

No matter what manner of circumstance others may work against us to induce us to believe we can alter the form of our original traditions, we must willingly allow the spirit of our Ancestors to bind our practice of their way to us.   Nothing else is relevant.

In this effort, we can *never* overemphasize the importance of tradition.   Our traditions are all that has come to work for us.   They reflect our human essence, our interpretation of the Universe and are the most apparent manifestation of our asilic and cultural imperatives.

We should know better than to continue to believe the "truth" of liars.   At what point in our relationship with chronic, psychopathic liars do we start to believe them?   At what point do we come to accept something that normatively characterizes them, which they have been working so hard to euroversalize, i.e., project onto others, as normatively characterizing us.   We should be able to see that to even entertain this arrogant white supremacist propaganda is to promote the barefaced lie of our ancestors' intellectual inferiority.

The other side of the euroversalism argument, that one which is put forth by the "liberal" western scientific community, must also be put to rest in the Afrikan mind.   We cannot buy into the "human universal" analysis that makes the european thought and behavior normal, although momentarily aberrant somewhere in the distant past.   This argument gives the impression that the European's social and cultural development was the same as all others.   Therefore, believing this, we can but conclude that at one time they were one with the Creator, the Universe, humanity and Nature – a very dangerous proposition and debilitating position for any thinking Afrikan to take.

Technology

Thinking Afrikan must stop equating the idea of what is "modern" with that of progress. The changes people produce over time to enhance their knowledge, comfort and sense of security are primarily technological in nature. They are simply different *ways* of doing what has always needed to be done, i.e., different techniques. They are not changing what needs to be done, only how what needs to be done is done. Technology is technology, whether ancient or contemporary.

When it comes to technology, the true measure of importance is the spirit of its application. We have to stop creating erroneous parallels between the idea of advanced technology and the so-called western genius, making them necessarily one and the same.

In the same way, we have to overcome our fixation on "modern," as if it is anything other than a haughty eurocentric temporal designation. It is nothing more than a word Europeans have formulated to indicate the present time/reality. Even though the word in itself my be harmless, its political connotations are devastating for anyone not classified as white or European. We have to stop equating the contemporary world order with a liberating, progressive superiority[101] and the past with a stifling, regressive inferiority. We have to stop presuming, as their evolutionary theories force us,[102] that later or more means better.

Healing Internal Ruptures

In the Center, Afrikans exist in a space where they do not have to live like those beyond its borders. We can be who we are with each other. In these centers of Afrikan community, we can be our traditional selves. We do not have to be concerned about the intrusion of those who are willfully in direct conflict with universal order. In becoming our Ancestors, we know that "order is the first law in heaven."[103]

We follow our tradition. And, traditionally, our social life operated within the rules of the Universe. Centers must be spaces where trust and Afrikan self-expression is common and communal. "One's society should be a source of strength, not a constant drain on one's energies and self-confidence."[104]

It should go without saying that warriors should not consciously deceive other Afrikan people of good character and intent. How can people who call themselves revolutionaries be successful in their work if they make a practice of deceiving themselves, each other and those for whom they say they would lay down their lives? Regardless of the level of deceit religiously practiced among the creators of and adherents to the aberrant reality many of us choose to remain hostage to, that way of thinking, speaking and doing is unAfrikan. It works to intensify our fragmentation.[105]

> In African tradition, speech, deriving its creative and operative power from the sacred, is in direct relation with the maintenance or the rupture of harmony in man and the world about him. That is why most traditional oral societies consider lying as an actual moral leprosy. In traditional Africa the man who breaks his word kills his civil, religious and occult person. He cuts himself off from himself and from society. Better for him to die than to go on living, both for himself and for his family....When a man thinks one thing and says another he cuts himself off from himself. He breaks the sacred unity, the reflection of cosmic unity, creating discord in and around him.[106]

Lying to others within the community is bad enough. But lying to oneself about oneself is about the most damning thing that a person can do. This is delusional.

Still, lying to those one is sworn to protect and whose shoulders brace yours on the frontline is tantamount to treason. And, if you will deceive yourself, you will deceive them. Know that not speaking truth, i.e., being silent and/or letting lies circulate unchecked, is still lying. We have to remember that Ancestral wisdom that "where there is no shame there is no honor." And, if nothing else, our warriors must be honorable.

Nonetheless, conscious Afrikans, regardless of their level of commitment or approach to nationbuilding, are not the only ones we have to think about when considering this truth. There are always those with genocidal intent toward Afrikan people. Among them are those who smile and want to converse with us, who lie to us in order to access our truths. Often, without speaking, they betray themselves. This also applies to those of us who seek out their company. We must be observant of relations beyond the Zone of Modulation.

After all this time, we should know what lies beneath that smile. "Smiling faces tell lies."[107] For us, relative to them, the best advice has already been given by our Ancestors. The Yoruba tell us that "one does not discuss secret matters in the presence of a tattler" and that "a treacherous person is not someone to tell profound matters to." The Ethiopians warn that "confiding a secret to an unworthy person is like carrying grain in a bag with a hole." When dealing with our adversaries, a mask of deception is appropriate. Do not be dismayed or hampered by the fact that, in a society of liars, in a reality where everyone is kept in check against critiquing others by their personal history of lies, "a truthful person is hated."[108] Speak truth to those with the capacity to respect it for what it is.

Honesty is not something warriors offer their enemies. Enemies, no matter the circumstances, no matter the stipulations or benefits, should never be given the unspoken respect of friends. That does not mean that enemies cannot be exploited for their strategic and tactical secrets. It only means that you should *never* be honest with them about anything of significance. Deal with enemies as necessity dictates.

On this point, a number claiming warriorhood, but who are determined to keep Yurugu at their center no matter the cost, use eurisms[109] as excuses to keep the company of their destroyers. A pathetic example of this is seen among those pretend warriors who defend their enemy-loving antics with the trite yurugian battle cry "Keep your friends close, but your enemies closer." In most of these cases, this is an intentional engineering of european thought to their advantage by weak-minded individuals who are aware enough of the consequences of their deception, if found out, to feel the need to rationalize their desire to keep company with Europeans, while still trying to hold on to a warrior's honor.

When we know the intent of the european mind, this instruction to "befriend" one's enemy means to study those close enough to know and sabotage any such efforts beforehand. It means to stay knowledgeable of your enemies' capabilities and operations. There is no intention to cultivate friendships or alliances based on mutual respect or interests. As with other Machiavellian convictions,[110] it is a popular eurism of those who are always either engaged in war or excitedly harboring an expectation of its perpetual imminence. It is an insecure aggressor's philosophy. Why else would a cold-blooded, supremacist imperialist want to keep an enemy closer, except to play with them?

We should be especially careful of those contradictory Afrikan "warriors" who tactically espouse this philosophy because their most heartfelt loyalties are highly questionable. In the critical assessment of who stands by our side and what they will do in the face of an enemy, it should go without saying that "If you know who his friends are, you know who he is."[111] If asked about our position on this matter, we need only speak the wisdom of our Ancestors who tell us that "a wise man seeks a friend, a fool seeks an enemy."[112]

Knowing the hell most of us have experienced to become Afrikan, another pressing question arises around the issue of deceit. How does a warrior who has come into his or her Afrikan self, an Afrikan recovering from european addictions, who, therefore, has led a life of deceit, deal with her or himself and the conscious community honestly? Deeply imbedded personality defense mechanisms take time to recognize, stop and reverse.

Because we know mentacide's strength, even in the minds of those who have developed an incredible knowledge of self, and we know that "to fall and rise up again is the journey of this world,"[113] the answer is fairly simple. You do this as earnestly as your spirit will allow with those striving to be Afrikan like yourself. And you never forget that you must exercise the greatest of patience with self.

Here, though, more than anything else, we are speaking about working on correcting the terror that a life of contradictory thought, word and behavior has wreaked on our minds. Sometimes, warriors intent on being Afrikan feel that they are in a battle for their sanity against themselves. That voice and video projector in their heads seem to be on auto pilot, determined to force them to return to the narcotized comfort of insanity brought by non- and anti-Afrikan thoughts and images.

At times, it can be most distracting and demoralizing, having to spend so much energy fighting against an insanity-driven, rogue mind. Even worse, as we progressively become more Afrikan centered, this "mind," which in european psychobabble might be called the "other-directed"- or shadow-ego, becomes more tenacious and belligerently disrespectful. It becomes like a parasitic, bad habit desperately clinging to its formerly compliant host.

The effective transformation of lost souls (and other confused types) into warrior scholars tells us to take this desperation as a sign of impending doom for that evasive, uninvited and unwelcome ego and victory for our ReAfrikanizing spirit. Its escalating reactions to our fight for psychological liberation signal its recognition that the tables have turned. It has become aware that it is under assault by an assertive, awakening Afrikan consciousness. Yet it remains, in the same way as Yurugu reacts to the growing evidence that his empire is falling apart all about him, determined to maintain its consciousness-sucking hold over us.

It may be comforting to know that these disturbances in your steady movement toward Afrikan peace will begin to dramatically decrease with every focused effort you make to wean yourself of european insanity. Affirmations of the warrior scholar you aspire to be, repeated with each annoying interruption, are effective defenses against depression or relapse.[114] Call on your higher self to elevate you above that which is less than you. Bear in mind Nana Garvey's instruction to "let no voice but your own speak to you from the depths" and you will be safe and unhampered in your journey home. His wisdom must be made operational in the deepest recesses of your consciousness if you are to truly be free as a warrior scholar.

Lastly, do not fault yourself for this difficulty. It comes with the territory of ReAfrikanization. Recognize that, to some degree, all warriors are addicts recovering from eureason. Only a few of us were not at some point held captive by the drug of european insanity. In this wretched world, none remains unscathed. And with dealers and encouraging addicts all around, it is a habit hard to fully break. However, with a healing knowledge of self, sufficient doses of a warrior scholar's awareness and a loving, caring patience, in time, the distractions will end. You will again be free within yourself.

Still, with freedom comes awareness and responsibility of what one has been and needs to become. In this respect, the goal of the recovered warrior scholar is first to correct self and then daily expend the energy necessary to correct the damage we have done to the community. This can only be done through working to reverse the insanity we saw in ourselves in other awakening Afrikans.

The Question of All-Inclusiveness

We also have to remember that Yurugu has severely

weakened the most fundamental of social adhesives securing us to each other – our sense of naturally trusting each other.   This, now internalized shortcoming, works even more against us the longer we feel powerless and the deeper we become entrenched in the competitive, adversarial games of western society.   For, increasingly, it continues to do all it can to even further divide us along any fissures it can create which lead us to view each other with increasing skepticism and, eventually, as incompatible, antagonistic aliens.

We must overcome this fault if we are to be victorious. But this illness cannot be cured by blindly adhering to any political philosophy requiring everyone to be included in our revolutionary army, regardless of their politics.   That would present us with an even worse downfall.

Our people's mentacide is deep.   It is so consuming in some that they want anything but to be Afrikan.   Others harbor a mentacide that is even more detrimental because it is concealed under the cloak of an Afrikan center.   These are those who claim Afrikan origins and loyalties but who have fully committed themselves to die before they would forego or shed their european ways and appetites for a more righteous, disciplined way.

It is in members of this more dangerous group where we find treason most subconsciously practiced.   They are the true agents of whiteness because of their subterfuge.   They would have us redefine the original Afrikan in the european's image.   And this would include, but is not limited to, personality, way of thinking, family disorders, beliefs, tastes and sexual confusions.   They carry the seeds of this contagion with them always.[115]

Revolutions that require every "Afrikan," including those who consciously see our enemies as their eternal ally and work to promote and protect any enemy's subversive interests among our people, do not succeed.   At most, saboteurs such as these systematically work to smother revolutionary efforts until the real oppressing forces are able to finally coopt or destroy them. Within the context of western imperialism, whether occurring among the oppressor or the oppressed, *no* revolution has ever included everyone.

Revolutionaries will hear three myths [116] which can seriously erode their morale. One is that you can never remove your enemy. Another is the assumption that a revolution cannot occur without a general consensus at the grassroots level. And the third misconception, about which we just spoke and which is directly tied to the second, is that revolutions must include everyone in order to be successful. The latter is the most damaging assumption of the three because it implies that the revolution cannot possibly become successful without including those of us who have a vested interest in being European, as well as those who may not want to be them but still live for their love and validation. Together, these two groups add up to the vast majority of Afrikans in this society. Since this discussion has already begun, we will deal with this last myth first.

How quickly we forget, in the effort to move in any direction signaling the possibility of empowerment, that revolution has never been an option for negroes. "A domesticated dog does not know how to hunt."[117] It only knows how to beg. In Kelly Miller's words, "the negro pays for what he wants and begs for what he needs."

A nonconfrontational compliance with their oppressors is their innately fundamental political philosophy. They can only act against their own.[118] That is the ingrained nature of the negro.

Sure, they would love to talk with you about the "Black problem" under the pretense of group solidarity. But it is only to distract you from your purpose with protracted, meaningless, barren debate, thereby earning themselves invaluable brownie points from their sworn masters. When you get caught up in the issues and lives of those members of our community who absolutely do not want to change into someone better, you find yourself riding a counterrevolutionary treadmill. To blindly embrace those with a deep commitment to their self-defeating philosophy simply because it is phrased in the spirit of humanity or brings us together momentarily as a people is ludicrous if we wish to independently empower an Afrikan nation.

You do not embrace those who will take you straight to hell, no matter how much blood you share with them. Some will never listen. Everyone is not able to see. And, most importantly, it is not healthy to keep the company of people who proudly wear the scars of the generations of their physical and mental rape.

There are casualties in every war. The conversion of negroes is not of interest or a goal for Afrikan warrior scholars, regardless of the potential based on them being born of Afrikan lineage. Some in our community have a vested interest in not being Afrikan. So, the idea that finding meaningful, incompatible differences among Afrikans only serves to further divide and weaken us, but does not take into account the fact that there are people within our group who must be routed out in order for us to make Afrikan progress and, eventually, become one. It misses the point that this is already the case, and has been so for quite a while now.

You cut the infectious animal from the herd. You don't keep it there just for numbers. Progress cannot occur by embracing enemies within.

The need to include everybody in our war, especially those who boast about subsisting in the deepest states of mentacide, who hate the idea that someone might think that somewhere in them there might be anything recognizable as Afrikan, is extremely problematic. If we have to get over anything it is the idea that it is necessary to bring everybody into the fold in order to win. This is the diversity sham working its finest magic on the minds of those Afrikans seeking an easy way to peace.

It is the idea that everyone of Afrikan descent must be brought into the decision making fold because we think we are a democratic family. It intentionally forces us to overlook the fact that there are those in our family who hate us. The diversity sham operates on the principle that you cannot make revolutionary progress without everyone included. It is so easy to become completely misdirected when believing that everybody must be together in order to return home.

The second misconception we need to correct is that revolutionary, guerrilla actions do not have the possibility of success without the general support of the dispossessed masses. This is a reasonable conclusion, given that munitions, supplies, food and information are transported to and from the frontlines by "civilians." Moreover, many of the residences of these transporters provided safe havens for the escape and rest of guerrillas. However, while it is true that most past and present guerrilla activities have the tacit support of the majority of the oppressed population, this is neither an absolute nor a requirement for successful guerrilla activities, military, intellectual or otherwise.

When the majority of the oppressed are too afraid or culturally misoriented to consider liberation as a viable option, especially, where freedom and independence are believed to have already been achieved (whether in the form of a "kinder/gentler" oppression or a total absence of it), then their support is highly unlikely. And, in many ways, what they may naively conceive of as help can be very dangerous to the health and welfare of revolutionaries seeking their assistance. Tattletelling is a normal response from the frightened against those who would free them from the mortified safety of oppression. In these cases, as is plainly the case for warrior scholars in this society today, the requirement of popular support for rebellion flies in the face of reality. Of course, for these warrior scholars, the other option, resignation to alienation, makes even less sense.

In such a situation, the warrior scholar must be content with the knowledge that standing as a revolutionary example, regardless of the absence or presence of allied righteous minds and bodies is enough. Such selfless thought and action, once momentum for it is gained, will serve to dramatize the rhetorical contradictions of the oppressor. In dire political situations, sometimes the only possible way that a people can be awakened to their unrecognized plight is through the courageous and determined exercise of power by a few. Revolutionary workers must become these catalysts, for only by example will the revolutionary spirit spread from one or a small group of revolutionaries to the people.

For those already accustomed to their fear, for those who have already resigned themselves to a vanquished, fragmented invisibility and have no reason to question their intended destruction, a real and genocidal assault against their being must be proven again and again and again. It must be demonstrated to them to the point where it significantly, detrimentally and openly impacts their lives. Only then would they consider going against those from whom they have spent lifetimes seeking love and validation.

Revolutions can occur without a general consensus at the grassroots level, but only through the sustained, sacrificial effort of a few who know that their mission is to open the eyes of those among their people who have the capacity to see. But they must open their eyes themselves. We do not beg. We set the standard which others can see and choose to follow, if they are intrepid enough.

The third of these fallacious assumptions is that you can never remove (kill off) your enemy. This carries the same manipulative intent as the instruction of master thieves that you should not steal or you will go to hell. Accepting it, one is defeated before one begins. If one has been systematically assaulted by a sworn enemy since the point of first contact, and there is no possibility of honest negotiation because history has proven that this sworn enemy has done nothing but lie in dealing with others, then the choices are obvious – destroy or be destroyed.

Some may say that destruction is a harsh option, given the possibilities of containing enemies or attaining a balance of power.   These two alternatives become no more than temporary shackles from which the eternal destroyer would eventually return victorious, something history bears out so well.   And, it is because of this that many warrior scholars have come to the logical conclusion that there is but one "final solution"[119] to this Afrikan problem.

Most interestingly, Europeans are doing just what they are telling us we cannot.   Their assault on Afrikan people is genocidal.   If we just momentarily look at history, we see a record where peoples were systematically exterminated by them.   They tirelessly work to remove (kill off) their enemies.

Two of the better known examples are of the Taino[120] and the Tasmanians,[121] who no longer exist.   These enemies of Yurugu were physically removed from planet Earth by the violence of the european mind and hand.

We hear, time and time again, the Afreason[122] that you always give your enemy an out because you cannot (should not) kill them all.[123]   It is in our nature to be sympathetic, even in the closing of a victorious response to a horrific attack against us.   But, again, our current environment is not traditional Afrika and we are not dealing with Afrikan people.   The rules of combat which apply to the Afrikan reality do not apply in this insecure, barbaric, immoral alien one.   These are two irreconcilably different worlds.   And, before we engage our enemies in combat again, this lesson must be learned.

Unless we are talking of "enemy" in the generic sense of always having someone who is at odds with you, then the enemy can be removed.   Of course, we know that this "generic" intent is not what they mean.   This rhetorical ethic is no more than a military ploy designed to circumscribe the Afrikan warrior scholar's mind.

The New Vanguard

We should make a mission/crusade of warning initiate

warrior scholars about what becomes of those with good intentions who naively answer the call of such an ostensibly sympathetic, all-embracing political philosophy that espouses that a revolution cannot occur without everyone's consent. They have to be taught about those among us who despise us and who will never cease working to destroy any effort to organize Afrikans around Afrikans, even while loudly professing an undying commitment to the Afrikan revolution.

Inexperienced, impressionable students of the Afrikan Way must be told to vigilantly look out for impostors. We should make no assumptions about what they know about those who are with us only to be against us.

Even having delivered the word, our response to this threat within cannot stop there. We, ourselves, must take it upon ourselves to identify and rout out any and all individuals and groups who profess Afrikan ideologies but systematically corrupt what is Afrikan with what is innately others. Particularly among these treasonous pretenders are those who work so hard to graft european abnormalities onto Afrikan traditions so that they, and the Yurugu they have deified, can appear normal.

Our reinforcements must be made aware that everyone does not now and may never have the spiritual or mental capacity to be Afrikan. It must be made clear to them that they are fighting to rebuild an Afrikan protected, solvent reality for those Afrikans who want to be Afrikan. They must be made aware that not everyone understands, or even wants to understand, what we are trying to build. Many, who look like us, see us as enemy and will resist our empowerment to the death.

This is a righteous vision. And it only awaits our spiritual, psychological and physical rescue. No one else can pry our liberation out of the deadly grip of western culture and society. There is no doubt that such an incredible war effort will require all of our experience, the New Vanguard's energy and more from Spirit than we have ever called forth, for what began against us with the first invasion of our motherland will not be brought to an end in our time.

Collective Villages

Spiritual, intellectual and physical warfare begins and gains momentum within small collectives. Our collectives are composed of individuals consciously aware of the challenge of their difference from Isfet[124] and secure in their Ma'atian[125] vision. These communities or, rather, villages, are already located throughout the Motherland and Diaspora. They form the nuclei of our nationbuilding effort. They are Centers, our Centers.

By now, we should be able to recognize the immensity of our struggle to regain ourselves as an Afrikan people and the forces which are quickly mobilized against any highly visible, relatively unsophisticated,[126] massive nationbuilding effort by us. Because we recognize this, it only makes sense now, even this late in the game, that we must start small and sure. A brief ourstorical glance backward shows us that public advertising, mass organizing, loud voices and flamboyancy have done little but serve undisciplined, overambitious, individual egos. As history easily bears out, these activities do little more than set us up as easy targets for the predators from the Caucasus caves and their allies by alerting them to what we are thinking and doing beforehand. Therefore, we know that, if we are to be successful in this crucial endeavor, we must quietly do the work of building the foundation of a nation that will gradually close ranks through the coming generations.

We build centers of power, clean, clear and efficient in the collective vision and missions of the individuals involved. We do the substantial, formative work of ReAfrikanization and nationbuilding within these centers of power. What we build serves as models for other potential centers to emerge and take their deserved places within the progressively evolving Ma'atian reality of conscious Afrikan people.

It is no secret that the struggle toward building an Afrikan nation will be a long, arduous one. The wisdom of Afrika teaches us that when something is bent too far in the wrong direction it will have to be bent even farther in the right one in order for it to again become straight. This wisdom has also taught us that if we are to nationbuild correctly, if such a movement is to contain the concentrated fortitude and determination that make liberation a natural ideal, if it is honor that is truly to be earned and therefore deserving of the greatest protection, then it will be more than well worth the wait of the many generations that it will take to move families into communal villages then into clans/tribes then finally into one nation.

Study and Application

If we don't know ourstory, we are bound to repeat the same mistakes that have us pinned under the crushing misery we presently find ourselves. If we don't know the story of the line of our indefatigable nationbuilding revolutionaries, then we will make the same mistakes they made as they pursued revolutionary knowledge.

These Afrikans were not failures. They did not lose or give up. They are not to blame for the current state of the Afrikan nation. Quite the contrary, they set a standard we have yet to again reach. These undaunted warrior scholars are to be credited with our continuing existence as Afrikans. If anything can be credited with our current plight, it is us.

Though quite prematurely, subassimilationists are brazenly celebrating their victory over us while would-be warriors still remain ignorant of their life's work. But we, more than they, keep the Afrikan response to the onslaught of anti-Afrikan forces fixed in its developmental stages. We, the warrior scholars, those who know what has happened and what we are up against, are supposed, at least within our community, to have our traitors in check. It is us who should be supplying those coming behind us with a working knowledge of this war.

Those who recognize our movement as a protracted developmental stage know that a study of our ancestral revolutionaries is imperative if our response to the onslaught is to be victorious. We must study the trials, tribulations, accomplishments and visions of those who forever see us as a people, recognize we are at war with another people and not some arbitrary, impersonal politico-economic machine, who see the Creator in our genius and who do not give up. We must study the warriors who have earned our respect by "being closest to the enemy, *in pursuit.*"

We also have to realize that study must be coupled with praxis. It must find concrete expression through practical, studied application. There can be no separation of the two if we are to become a fully liberated, sovereign nation. We should not think without subsequently acting. And the results of our action should lead us to further critical thought about what best to *do* next.

Without ongoing, consistent, practical application of what we study, we become regressively sidetracked into an intellectualized, devolutionary coma that enables our enemies to gain even greater leverage over our freedom. When we become distracted in this way, the only time we seize is delusional. If we stop any meaningful revolutionary activities because we become lost in excessive, repetitive study of what we already know enough to act on, or study without using the lessons gained to improve the quality of our rebellion, others will be given the opportunity to move even farther forward against us simply employing actions they long ago learned should naturally accompany their study of how to best undermine the strategic conclusions we have yet to reach.

Only fools would believe others bent on our destruction stop when we do. Progressive movement requires a delicate, mutually benefitting and reinforcing balance between the energy put into thought and that placed in action.

And by no means should we, as critical Afrikan warrior scholars who are aware that everything is not as it seems, be indiscriminate about who we study in ourstory. "When the eyes come upon a matter, they must look hard and well."[127] We should know that indigenousness, lineage or renown do not automatically speak to Afrikan consciousness. We must be selective about who we study because not all revolutionaries are true warriors. Not everyone on a frontline is nationbuilding *for us*. Many were/are simply reactionaries with a subassimilationist end goal cloaked behind a loud, charismatic voice or image held up as symbolic of our strength and vision. We have seen the devastating effect of this on our movement.

So, this must be a critical study of revolutionary warfare. We cannot accept without qualification or ourstorical hindsight the beliefs, strategies/tactics or objectives of those who have been defined as revolutionaries. We have to question why leftist/marxist publishing companies (of the european nation of which they are inextricably a functional part) invest in publishing the words and stories of particular Afrikan, Asian and Hispanic/Latino writers, theoreticians, clergy and political figures. This is not rocket science. It does not require great intellectual insight or an expansive working knowledge of (revolutionary) history. The question is simple. How does what they say benefit and/or keep friendly their blue-eyed comrades?

Once determined to uncover the most uncompromised, comprehensive revolutionary Afrikan path, we need to be tough-minded enough to separate the actual valor, if any, of these role models from their image and ideology. And, in the same way, we need to be keen enough to differentiate their fundamental political objectives from the end goal of a sovereign, independent, empowered Afrikan nationhood.

This also means that we, as warrior scholars, must unequivocally reserve the right to dismiss from the revolutionary ranks anyone who, or any group which, has been propped up (by us or who knows who) but who is revealed to still speak and/or act in alien ways. We cannot afford to be waylaid by those subtly teaching or practicing a blackened marxism, sexual confusion or any other european fitting and benefitting ideological agenda any more than we can tolerate openly professing negroes. In fact, they would be worse because they are supposed to know better. Only those actively and consistently adhering to a philosophy of "Race First," personally *and* publicly are worth our time and energy.

Unfortunately, many aspiring to the frontline are often ignorant about the true character of those we have been taught to admire. Many of us who have these recognizable faces plastered on their clothes and walls have no idea what they did/do or were/are about. In many cases, we have simply been sold a snippet of an impressive image, e.g., a fist raised, a furrowed brow, a big afro or airborne locks, an unholstered weapon, and an equal dubious assumption of revolutionary consciousness.

We must reserve the revolutionary's right to continuous, unbridled truth. We have the right to change our minds about who leads us as we become more knowledgeable about who they are inside. People come into our lives for a reason, which is not always for more than a moment.

Therefore, there should be no sacred cows in our movements. In good conscience, we cannot unreflectively and, therefore, irresponsibly adhere to an "11th COMMANDMENT [which] states, "THOU SHALL NOT MAKE ANY CRITICISM OF POPULAR GROUPS, INDIVIDUALS, TENDENCIES AND IDEAS IN The MOVEMENT."[128]

It is recognized in our tradition that individuals, without a people's traditional guidance, can become lost. "The person who knew the way last year does not necessarily know the way this year."[129] At the same time, we know this is seldom the case for those who ask the way and even less so for those who ask our Ancestors.

Not questioning images in a reality dominated by subtle, subliminal cultural and political seduction allows the confusion inherent within their messages to grow. In such a world, the objectives of such images, whether elevated by them or us, carry a high probability of coming under the ideological direction of anti-Afrikan minds.

Those who earnestly fought for the liberation of our people are not the same as those who fought to reform a knowing, intentional european nation to their (individual) advantage. The latter build their final reputations on how well they work to endear or charm representatives of european power into accepting us as being intrinsically less, though outwardly equal. They fight for the attention and notoriety which will gain them higher access to the perks of racist imperialism. This is the negro's mission – to make the Afrikan more palatable to the pale mind.

Measuring the quality and worth of those we study (observe and/or read) and keep close to our warrior spirit should be based on how they articulate and act on an Afrikan vision for Afrikan people, i.e., how they envision and work toward a world of Afrikans returned to power with full remembrance (regardless of how limited or thorough their intellectual critique of the Maafa, our mentacide or those who have spoken, written and acted against us). In contrast, concern over the welfare of those who have instigated, perpetrated and benefitted from our fall, regardless of their stature, should not be our priority.

Those embracing a "we're all human" (humanist) ideology that is colorless, colorblind, deracialized genoculturally, and/or who disparagingly speak about our traditions as if the only path to success is to ape the european pattern or instruction of blind misdevelopment with only slight modifications here and there, should be dismissed for the european apologizing/defending advocates that they are. Critical questions must be subjectively addressed objectively[130] in the context of the question of nationbuilding.

We must ask ourselves why the leaders of Afrikan organizations would sleep with the enemy (in the presence of so much Afrikan intelligence and beauty) and how their political philosophy reflects this whoremongering mentacide. We must question the reason behind the reason that the political structures almost exclusively studied and advocated evolved in nonAfrikan cultural cradles. And, if Afrikan in origin, why study mutations or forgeries? Why not study the original?

We must ask ourselves who benefits from the economic order these "revolutionaries" have left largely unchanged since our enslavement and colonization. Why is Afrika still economically frustrated and unprotected? An equally important question is of what "leaders" have carved out for their individual selves in defending raw capitalism's ongoing scramble for Afrika while proclaiming socialism/communism. We must ask why, in their claim to having achieved a respectable level of self-definition for us, is the education of Afrikan children still being defined in terms of european trivia and "progressive" technological imperatives.[131]

With reference to those who have helped define revolutionary ideologies and lesson plans, there is also the question of personal loyalties. Their gift of oral or written articulation that may make some thoughts clearer or more appealing (though not unique) cannot be allowed to override any serious faults relative to truly being Afrikan. We should feel free to take from their study what makes sense and leave the rest to rot in the desert they so love. There is no reason I am aware of that should lead us to believe that our measurement of any of their revolutionary stances should in any way, shape, form or fashion be disconnected from their personal choices in mates, sexstyle and community of residence. We must know those who we select as models to emulate.

"Cultural Misorientation"

The number of Afrikans organized into our revolutionary centers must also be small as the result of the quality of consciousness in the general Afrikan community. The limited number of conscious Afrikans is borne out in the conclusions Kobi K.K. Kambon reached in his study of cultural misorientation.

Cultural misorientation is the outcome of losing one's sense of self. As the term implies, the members of a group, in this case Afrikans, are looking outside themselves, toward others, for their truth, explanations of reality and examples of whom they should be. Through every manner of forced conversion, we have been forced to dismiss and ignore what we have known as truth and identity and seek out our definitions of what constitutes reality, what we should aspire to in this reality and who we are as individuals and a people using the guide from not only an alien culture, but also a people who see us as the enemy.

> The obvious form of the contradiction is that it represents an African person functioning Eurocentrically, or according to the European survival thrust (i.e., an African displaying anti-African/European-centric functioning and behavior). Such Africans, for all practical purposes, then, think, feel and act like Europeans (they operate according to the European survival thrust). They are defined as normal and healthy by the European Worldview, because this worldview defines and reinforces only the European survival thrust. Culturally Misoriented Africans do not by and large experience any unusual anxiety or confusion (within the parameters of a Eurocentric consciousness) over their sense of identity or their functioning, because Eurocentric societal systems fosters this psychopathological condition among Africans. Psychological/Cultural Misorientation, therefore, refers to a grossly psychopathological condition in Africans which masquerades as functional normalcy within the framework of the alien Eurocentric-American societal system.[132]

In other words, when we look at who we have become through their psychopathic, racist vision of us, our insanity is made to appear normal.

I'm sure most of us have met or known Afrikan people who show no evidence of an Afrikan self anywhere. There was nothing in their walk, talk, voice, manner, associates, interests, style, loyalties, thought/analysis and, especially, eyes that spoke to having an Afrikan essence. In fact, all about them pointed toward the extremes of anti-Afrikanity. These individuals had been so fully assimilated into the european ethos,[133] had so become the European they loved and worshiped more than life itself, that they had literally lost themselves.

Even when forced to live amongst us, they see no connection with the rest of us. They have no recognition of us as family. I imagine, if they had their druthers, as most of the Afrikan characters in George Schuyler's *Black No More*,[134] they would do anything, including selling their soul (something many europeanized Afrikans see having as a negative stereotype for Afrikans anyway) to be visibly white in physical appearance. These individuals are examples of what we find at the farthest end of the range of the cultural misorientation continuum.

In a chart showing the distribution of Afrikans along this cultural misorientation (CM) continuum, Kambon cogently argued that approximately five to fifteen percent of us fall within this extreme, or what he appropriately calls the "Severe CM"[135] end of the distribution. At the other end of the spectrum are those with the least amount of confusion about their Afrikanity. Here, in what he has labeled the "Minimum CM"[136] category, somewhere between five and ten percent of us fall. In the middle, or "Moderate CM"[137] range, seventy to eighty percent of us lie. For conscious Afrikans seeking to assess the psychological state of our people, his graph provides an instructive, statistically based, normal bell shaped curve illustrating the concentrations of Afrikans along the continuum of a scientifically plausible distribution of Afrikans from the fully to mildly mentacidal. This was Kambon's original argument. And it was sound.

Progression or, rather, regression in the culturally misoriented state of Afrikan people has caused him to modify the proportionate concentrations of minimally, moderately and severely affected Afrikans in this curve. He has changed the severe percentage to between fifteen and forty, the moderate to between thirty and fifty and the minimum to between five and fifteen. Even with an increase of those of us falling within the Minimum CM category, this is a very, very significant regression.[138]

> Here we can observe a much bleaker picture reflecting a strong shift toward the Moderate-Severe to Severe end of the CM continuum (with the greatest shift being toward the Severe CM level)....This means, more or less, that Severe CM has overtaken Moderate CM to a large extent in the characterization of contemporary Black mental health in America based on the CM Paradigm. Hence, the risk factors for CM have probably soared upward over the past two decades with the advent of a generation of young Africans in America who have experienced virtually total racial integration throughout most aspects of their lives (particularly their entire formal-public lives). While being saturated with racial integration (which is tantamount to the imposition of Eurocentric cultural assimilation), this generation has had little-to-no African-centered institutional experiences to buffer and/or counter the unbridled European worldview onslaught upon the contemporary African psyche....As was indicated earlier, virtually all aspects of the lives of contemporary African youth and young adults are saturated with the European worldview, and thus their indoctrination to the European Survival Thrust.[139]

Kambon clearly demonstrates the degree to which this has happened in what I like to refer to as the *curve of consciousness*.

As warrior scholars, however, we should appreciate the fact that we are not dealing with even what might be considered an historically "normal" situation of oppression. So, we are not quite discussing a "normal" curve of mentacide. Rather, the curve that identifies the concentration and range of Afrikans in European society from the sane to insane is more of an abnormal shaped curve skewed in favor of the extremely mentacidal. The percentages of us who fall into the "Severe" and "Moderate" categories are greater just based on the extreme level of insanity incorporated into Afrikans socialized into Western society in the first place.

In addition, I have taken the liberty of modifying this tail[140] to reflect the rising warrior class. The "lump" that I have placed at the end of the tail of the "predicted distribution" of Afrikans on Kambon's cultural misorientation table represents the proportion of Afrikans who are (or are rapidly moving), in effect, beyond the pale of cultural misorientation or misalignment. It reflects the portion of us who have kept all of our appointments, attended all of our sessions and faithfully followed the healing advice of our ancestral naturopaths. It is within this "lump" where we find those deeply thinking Afrikans who constitute our Center.

The dotted curve representing this modification changes the severe, moderate and minimum percentages to, sixty, twenty-five and ten, respectively. It goes even further though, because the "lump" adds a range for those Afrikans who are not culturally misoriented. This lump is formed out of approximately five percent of those Afrikans we recognize as conscious. None of these Afrikans, internally or externally, exhibit any significant degree of those eurocentric characteristics held so belovedly by vanquished Afrikans.

Nonetheless, my difference with Kambon's estimates is only minor. A percentage here or there is not of consequence in the grand nationbuilding blueprint. Both he and I are speaking of a trend, an ongoing escalation in the proportion of

Cultural Misorientation Distribution for Afrikans

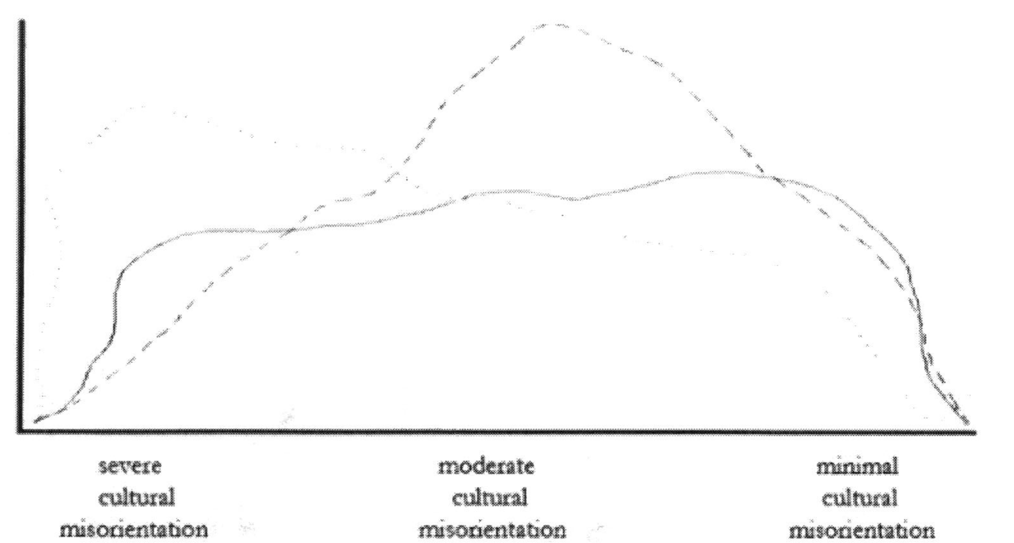

the Afrikan population suffering from intense levels of mentacidal self-hatred. That is the bigger picture.

The pace of our europeanization is increasing. Of this there is no question. And this increase is clearly wreaking more and more havoc on more and more Afrikan minds. In this respect, Kambon's model is a superb illustration of why centered Afrikans are automatically defined as insane within a eurocentric cultural paradigm, and we are, relatively speaking, steadily shrinking in numbers.

However, I would also contend that, as proportionately small as we may be in comparison to those aggressively pursuing their cultural misorientation, our mere existence is an incredible statement of our inner strength. That there are a number of us who have broken this mentacidal cycle is phenomenal. We thrive even when exposed to weakening, eurocentric models of socialization in a completely anti-Afrikan cultural context and society.

I argue that there are those of us whose intent is fully Afrikan. For us, there is no longer a "preponderance of European-centered beliefs, values, and attitudes in [our] functioning and behavior." [141]   Nor is there a reactionary rejection of european people. We have gone beyond remission to being healed, beyond any desire to return to the torment of self-denial, self-hatred and progressive disempowerment.

Ours is an active understanding of Yurugu, and anyone else who acts against us, as our enemy. It has become impossible for us to recognize ourselves as anything other than the workers of our people and fulfillers of our Ancestors' vision of Afrikan redemption. We openly acknowledge our righteous rage and believe in and affirm justice. Our "African Self-Consciousness" (ASC) (that personal sense of being Afrikan which molds and is molded by our physical and cultural environments) and our "African Self-Extension Orientation" (ASEO) (that untouchable, inborn, spiritual, asilic essence which urges us toward, and shows us how to be, our Afrikan selves) are in absolute harmony.[142] For that select few of us, there is no detachment between who we are here and who we are in the Universe. And room must be made for us in Kambon's model.

For those about whom I am speaking, even if a smidgen of the european demon rises from the depths to trouble our Afrikan peace of mind, it is just as quickly returned straight to its rightful hell by our uncompromising Afrikan intent. Just as eurocentric thought and behavior, adopted for whatever temporary reason, can unwittingly become our generalized norm so, too, can Afrikan centered thought and behavior, forcibly and consciously adopted in an effort to route out alien practices and thinking, become our whole way. For us, being Afrikan, to the full extent our collective Afrikan knowledge allows, has become real in its spiritual, mental and physical consequences. And, to be Afrikan, is to wholly reject the european way, divesting ourselves of every one of its worthless qualities.

Of all the terms we can use to describe the state of mind of Afrikans who culturally see themselves as Europeans, mentacide [143] is the most revealing because of its deadly denotation. Even so, cultural misorientation, zombiism, cultural suicide and other like terms carry equal descriptive weight and vary only slightly in definition. So, while in this work we are generally using mentacide to label this phenomenon, its explanation, for all intents and purposes, is synonymous with that of those like cultural misorientation. The psychic trauma they quite accurately describe is the same. Each critiques its equally devastating effect on Afrikan people.

Nonetheless, when taken separately for their face value meanings, cultural misorientation and cultural suicide are quite useful. As we understand it, cultural misorientation implies that the individual or group is wrongly oriented. They are facing away from *and act against* their native culture and toward/for that of alien invaders. They have been pointed in the incorrect direction for self instruction.

Cultural suicide introduces more of a conscious action

to one's mentacide in that a conscious effort is being put into killing the native culture in oneself. It is descriptive of an action initiated externally but completed internally. At the individual level, "subtle suicide" [144] is also a very useful, accurate descriptive concept to consider when explaining the symptoms of the method within the madness evidenced by the drive to self-destruction arising from a deeply ingrained self-hatred.

Progress

We are warrior scholars in recovery from addictions to pale appetites. As such, we are still susceptible to the demoralizing tow of propaganda specifically directed against our efforts toward liberation.[145] Therefore, we must take care to reconceptualize how we measure our progress so that it positively reflects this imbalance to our advantage. Everything is relative. So, this measurement must be grounded in our assessment of the relative psychological density or fluidity of those who occupy the layers of our Centers.[146]

Sometimes, it may appear that all our revolutionary struggle is for naught.[147] It may appear as if Europeans are still effortlessly winning over the minds of Afrikan people, while we are struggling to maintain the attention of our own children. We, ourselves, may also unwittingly fall victim to the morale battering of a thoroughly anti-Afrikan society that has severely infected those who most need to heed our warnings.

We can find ourselves resigning, feeling that we are doing no more than documenting our demise as we speak Afrikan truth to and about our people. Often we come to this conclusion when writing or speaking revolutionary truth because we are unable to find evidence of any immediate or emerging change or positive growth in those who claim that they are listening. In fact, at times, despite our best efforts, our conditions and mentality can look as if they are worsening for the community as a whole.

However, deep down in our spiritual core, we know better. With studied hindsight, we know that change at the personal level, which precedes change at the communal level, is a slow progress. Afrikans knowledgeable of our legacy of effective struggle know that this progress must take into account the fact that mentacide is a progressive disease. And mentacide must first be slowed down, then stopped, and finally reversed. Becoming Afrikan is a transformation that is ongoing and generally takes many, many, many determined years.

So, before we judge other Afrikans or become impatient with family (especially those making a serious, concerted effort to understand what is wrong) we have to ask ourselves how long it took us to progress to this point on our path. With sincere empathy, we have to humbly make the effort to look deeply inside to see just how very far we have yet to go.

In our reactionary despondency over our generally collective submission to eurocentric style progress, we also have to recognize that progress must be redefined. On the one hand, we know that being a shadow of the European means that we are moving in the direction that european culture is willing us. However, on the other hand, we must understand that not moving in that direction does not mean we are standing still or failing.[148] Instead it means that we are *progressing* in another direction.

Simply rejecting european culture and society *is* progress. And the more forceful and determined the rejection, the greater the advancement away from yurugu's reality. The problem here for most of us is that we are measuring our advancement based on our perception of the failure of the Afrikan community in general to detach and distance itself from the european mainstream. Even though the western media are currently the primary causal agents, we see evidence of this "failure" at the personal, interpersonal and genocultural level in a wide variety of suicidal acts of self-hatred.

It manifests in subtly suicidal acts such as bad diet, drugs and alcohol, physical inactivity, violence, over consumption, kwk, set in motion by our interpretation of reality through the eyes of our enemies. It is the outcome of the genocidal acts systematically committed by others against us, such as disease, diseducation, encarceration, birth control, disarmament, kwk. Many of us consistently overlook the fact that this "failure" is also propagated by the western media as the victory of western progress and the relative weakness and decline of our Afrikan foundations.

A more accurate, psychologically beneficial, Afrikan centered measurement of the progression or regression of the Afrikan centered community would be in seeing how far our thought and action are taking us away from where they want us to go. The greater the distance between us and their way, the greater our progress.

Afrikan centered progress is not complicated. When conscious, our rejection of them is an appreciation of us.

Most of us just do not know to interpret this deliberately rebellious movement as progress. Mainly, this is because, most often, Europeans still command the center of our interpretation of reality. We still base our success or failure on whether or not we think they are winning against us, not on whether or not we know we are winning against them. We forget that the Afrikan Way and the european way are irreconcilably different.[149] We forget that any Afrikan movement against them, away from them, is a progressive movement toward our empowerment.

Three profound thoughts come to mind when dealing with these sometimes debilitating distractions. First, a quote from an author unknown to me defines obstacles as the "things that you see when you take your eyes off of your goal." Second, an Ashante proverb directs us to "act as if it is impossible to fail." And, third, in the context of the specific role of warriors in the war for our solvency and humanity, the visionary Afrikan writer Ayi Kwei Armah guides us to see that:

Endless our struggle must seem to those whose vision

reaches only to the end of today[150]....The present is where we get lost – if we forget our past and have no vision of the future[151]....A healer needs to see beyond the present and tomorrow.   He needs to see years and decades ahead. Because healers work for results so firm they may not be wholly visible till centuries have flowed into millennia. Those willing to do this necessary work, they are the healers of our people.[152]

Afrikan progress entails empowerment.   And empowerment is a mental, physical and spiritual strengthening that parallels a decline in the european influence over our being. Ignoring for the moment the European's taste for using duplicitous manipulation, public demonization, institutionally sanctioned force and systematic, brutal, inhumane violence against those who refuse to mentacidally submit to their lies, the only way that strong, tradition honoring, self-defining Afrikan voices cannot be silenced is if they are completely independent of european sponsorship, censorship and, therefore, ownership.   To be Afrikan we must be free to do so.

Building Family Within

"Work makes marriage, family and community possible."

Elleni Tedla

As warrior scholars, we know the depth of mentacide within our families. And we know firsthand the joy and pain it brings. So we should not try to fool ourselves into thinking that we are the saviors of a people who are fully conscious of their physical, psychological and spiritual destruction but who are simply lacking in the will to liberate themselves. The vast majority of Afrikan people want nothing to do with anything Afrikan, [153] except it be neutered, despiritualized and sanctioned through Europeans by active or passive negroes, or other confused types. On this point, we must be truthful.

By virtually any observable measure, we, *as a people*, are losing. [154] "We are a vanquished nation...." [155] This is no shame. We did not understand the nature of our enemy. Most of us are still unable to fully psychologically grasp the living personification of Isfet. To do so would force us to go places, in defining what is and is not human, that we are not yet prepared to go. However, what is most shameful is that the number of us who have allowed ourselves to become duped into being the main collaborators in the conspiracy to commit genocide against ourselves is growing. This is a real and painful awakening for those of us who profoundly honor our Afrikanity.

As ReAfrikanized nationbuilders, we do not have to look around the world to see the fear, distrust, bewilderment and even hatred many chronically mentacidal Afrikans hold toward us. All we need do is look at our own families and see mentacide at work against us.

It is the repulsion that many of our immediate and extended blood relatives express toward us, and our understandable, genocultural need to maintain and be a part of and build family, that force many of us to build new non-natal family. We should not have to fight Europeans and family at the same time. For sane people, it is only reasonable to "want to work in a society [we] belong to, with friends moving in directions [we] can live with."[156]

When we feel the pain of disrespect, rejection and loneliness from those who should unconditionally love us, but qualify the giving of their love based on our willingness to commit treason against our Ancestors, we must be amenable to looking outside our immediate blood relatives for family. There is no Afreason as to why we should needlessly suffer in this way. The psychological tearing which can so easily result from being rejected by those who are supposed to love us no matter what should never be allowed to become so great that we are distracted from our nationbuilding work. When spurned by kin, we must find ways to create family with those we love, because they are Afrikan at heart and have chosen to walk this path along with us.

There is no reason for conscious Afrikans to suffer because we have chosen to be Afrikan. We should not have to be without a close knit collection of caring, reciprocating, sincere family simply because we choose to reject insanity.

Family, like the honored titles Mama, Baba, Sister, Brother, Asafo, Jegna, Elder, Ancestor, kwk. is an earned designation. It is an honor earned through a demonstrated, practiced love. "Just anyone is not another person's relative, one's relative is one that has done good to one."[157]

Blood relationship is too precious to be turned into a

weapon used to force people comply with the unreasonable. You do not keep relatives close hoping that this will keep them from mentally assaulting you. Duress should not be the motivational force binding unhealthy relationships. By default, a relationship is respectfully reciprocal. Having and keeping it is a privilege.

Certainly, blood will always be blood. Certainly, people should know the lineal story of their birth family so that they will know what to expect, suppress and elevate in themselves, their children, their grandchildren, kwk. But blood does not give our family members the right to make us feel less than they simply because conformity strokes their egos or makes them feel more secure. It should never be accepted as leverage in the hands of vanquished family members.

Centered Complementarity

In terms of finding complements and procreating family within the Center, the seasoned advice is "do your work" and what you seek will be found there.

> One other definite conclusion can be drawn from the collective revolutionary experience about the initial meetings that take place between two potential complements that lead to the development of lasting warrior relationships. They both tend to be doing their work when they first meet. This does not mean that they are oblivious to the need for companionship. It only means that finding a mate is not their sole priority or an overriding focus. Therefore, using this pattern as a guide, if you are doing your work, your study, your communal involvement, your communicating, attending to the needs of our people as a nation, your complement will be there also. You will find each other. Let your example be your attraction.[158]

In searching for our complements, though, we must be sure

about what we are doing and why we are doing it. There can be no uncertainty, for doubt undermines success.

Before we begin the search, though, we must ask ourselves "What does it take for (and from) one person to choose to confront madness?" "What does it take for (and from) an individual to confront an overwhelming assault against his or her being?" "What kind of inner strength is required for one to be willing to risk death to visualize and work toward a sane reality?"

Another critical question here is, "What does it take for two such individuals, each already individually assaulted beyond reason, to allow themselves to be targeted for even greater assault by yurugu's reality in an ongoing effort to extract themselves from insanity?" Even more critical a question is "Why would they be willing to procreate knowing full well the hateful, sustained assault that awaits the offspring they have sworn on their souls to provide for and protect." "What kind of commitment, strength and uncompromising vision does this goal of Afrikan family require of complements?"

Sustaining complementary relationships is no easy feat for warrior scholars. But a great deal of the battle is overcome when we have some idea about what to expect in our relationships. Love does not change the fact that we are at war. But, as much as is humanly possible, that war must be kept outside the sacred space which exists between us and our spouses and children.

This makes it imperative that we confront the erroneous idea that warrior couples must be hard to/on each other because they know nothing but fighting and violence. That is not us. That's the way of another people. That's the proven tradition of a nation of warmongers practicing their nature on each other, in every relationship, in every interaction. Like Malcolm, we can act in a warrior's way outside the home and be the loving, caring, humane people we naturally are inside of it.

Warrior couples are not new to us. Unlike our

homophilic, patriarchal enemies, we have always known and named our warrior men with their warrior complements and our warrior women with theirs. There was no Malcolm without Betty, no Fred without Akua (fka Deborah), no Medgar without Myrlie, kwk. Warrior complements must be politically in sync.

> A visionary aspect must appear in the relationship. The ability to plan for the future on the basis of a religious commitment to the Afrocentric worldview is the criterion of vision. Nothing can substitute for the visionary experience; it is the galvanizing element that keeps the relationship on track. To be able to ask, do you see and be assured that your partner does see the same vision provides a sense of communion. Commitment to a fundamental vision, a profound project, a spiritual quest, is the king of commitment which demonstrates vision. Relationships which are based on Afrocentric vision are never boring, dull, or without vitality. A visionary aspect to a relationship establishes a purpose outside of and beyond the daily considerations of living. The man and woman who dream together constitute the most advanced unit of an Afrocentric society.[159]

Only among those who have decided to internalize sexist, eurocentric ideologies do we find our complement Sisters missing. No feminist organization was needed for us to recognize the presence and power of our Sisters in arms. We have always known that "if a man sees a snake, and a woman kills it, what matters is that the snake does not escape."[160]

And, because so many of us have been driven into a state of planned confusion by the eureason embedded in the marrow of yurugian ideologies like this, we also have to deal with the misconception that the traditional Afrikan way of being complementary is an outdated, forced, emotionless reality harmful to the establishment of meaningful relationships in this so-called "modern, loving society." Both the interpretation of our complementary traditions and some newfangled humanity created by Yurugu are patently false.

Afrikan warrior women and Afrikan warrior men forming complementary relationships need to be comfortable with the fact that we are an emotional people. As warrior couples, our good health is dependent on our feeling the range of our emotional being, from the lightness of our happiness to the depth of each other's anger.

In a world where an alien reality conspires to force our anger into excessive and uncontrollable rages, there is a tendency toward imbalance within oneself and between self and complement. In reference to intimate relationships, the psychiatry of psychotics is the science of the unnatural idea that sexual aggression and competition are balance or normalcy. Accepting this abnormal thinking only opens the path leading us deeper into an uncontrollable, flesh-obsessed madness only satisfiable through the pursuit of insatiable, volatile, antagonistic, perverted appetites.

To return stability to our emotional being, we must return ourselves to an Afrikan reality. The social and cultural environment must be brought in line with who we are as individuals, complements, community and nation. Otherwise, as a rightly emotional people, we risk emotional desensitization (or oversensitization) and further entrapment in a rage that makes us other than who we are, unable to live together, unable to live long, whole lives. This requires a psychiatry which understands Afrikans as a people who cannot be themselves without a Sankofan return home.

Critical Capacity

Everyone makes mistakes. It's to be expected. "No single head can contain all wisdom,"[161] and "the wise man who ceases to learn ceases to be wise."[162] The person who does not spiritually and intellectually grow/improve is a person who does not learn from his or her mistakes. People who never experience consequences for their words or actions, be they negative or positive (or who only receive positive, or only negative, consequences regardless of what they have or have not said or done), lose their capacity to learn because they lose the ability to constructively accept and grow through criticism. They lose the ability to listen to anyone except themselves as knowledgeable or an authority, except to gain an advantage or avoid a punishment. Such a person cannot objectively look at self and is unable to consider the intent or truth of constructive criticism given to her or him. Such a person is ruled by a highly individualistic, self-centered ego.

In an egogenic society[163] acquaintanceship is upgraded to the level of friendship in the effort to accumulate more attention. And attention is something which readily, but mistakenly, becomes translated by such individuals as love. In such a reality, the fragility and struggle[164] of friendship causes the common sense of value and quality to take a back seat to obsessive fears of losing one's popularity through the threat of losing "friends." The innately quantitative nature of western culture forces one to work toward having as many "friends" as possible regardless of choices or outcome. Inevitably, everything in western society becomes reduced to the european mind's greatest common denominator – a count.

True revolutionaries know that a tested friend is a true friend. True friends would never move their friends away from righteousness by threatening to withdraw their friendship. And true friends always come in small numbers and without conditions, given the understood political parameters of those in the Center. As a child I was fortunate enough to be part of a community which imparted by word and deed the ancestral wisdom that a true friend is one who will tell you when you are wrong or mistaken and bring to your attention things that make you look bad, even at the possibility of losing your friendship. To this wisdom, we need to return.

Being a revolutionary requires a deep sense of humility and the ability to be righteous no matter whose feelings are at stake because being a revolutionary is an exercise in communal nationbuilding. It is an effort to gain and maintain consensus in direction. And such an underlying, community-guiding consensus requires an honest, tactful effort at expressing oneself and listening to others who have gained the right to be included in the community.

Morale

When most of what you seem to hear and see is bad news, shocking realizations about those around you who you thought were clear about their Afrikanity, painful news about those you honored because of their words and/or nationbuilding efforts that epitomized warriorhood, scary stories about "everyday" Afrikan people in mentacidal anarchy, and when what you hear and see is no exaggeration, what do you do to maintain your sense of direction and keep progressively moving forward? This is a question of morale. And it is a question asking how do warrior scholars, whose vision is not limited to their personal glorification and individualistic accumulation of knowledge, keep their morale when, seemingly, all around them there is nothing but deceit, suffering[165] and signs of military inferiority and vanquishment.

A defeatist attitude attends a logical consideration of the "fact" that Europeans have a massive destructive arsenal and means of gathering information. Propaganda is a weapon of war, though. Therefore, we cannot consider their truth in their terms.

There is no Afrikan logic in the eureason they spread across the battlefield. Their propaganda is meant to undermine the Afrikan possibility and break our will to exercise Afrikan power. A weapon's efficacy is relative to the user's vision and determination, not merely its destructiveness. How many times can we count our rising into victory in the face of being incredibly outnumbered and outgunned?[166] We know the answer to the question "What makes a soldier ride alone into battle?"[167]

Yurugian media outlets stages reality for those susceptible to their brainwashing. It is presented in such a way that their prey can come to no conclusion except that they will lose if they try to rebel against their oppression. Yet, too, there is an obvious factor that has stood the test of Afrikan time. Odds have never been a deterrent to a determined warrior.

Nothing is impenetrable. Nothing is indestructible. No people is irremovable from a tyrannical seat of power. No rule is unbreakable. Therefore, it is obvious that our fear is evident in our inaction. Ample evidence of this is recognizable in our self-destructive action also. These two reactions are the same. Knowing the deceit and dominative spirit of Europeans, warrior scholars holding a victorious vision for Afrikan people must determine what spiritual, mental and/or physical martial assault against this enemy can produce meaningful, progressive, cumulative damage now and/or later, rather than submit to defeat.

In general, though, loss of morale among warrior scholars is the result of a combination of factors, most of which can be found entangled in the social sediment all about us. It is the result of painful dejection and feelings of insecurity from those who should be closest to us in this fight. These demoralizing factors include:

- feelings of isolation and doubt as to one's individual capabilities,

- separation from birth family and peers (conscious and unconscious),

- questioning one's own rightness in the face of preponderant condemnation and denouncement by the majority of people, even Afrikans,

- feelings of being militarily overwhelmed and

- doubts about economic security and survival (for self and others in the community).

When issues of sanity and survival are in question, especially when we fear that what may be coming will undermine them even more, morality can reach an incapacitating nadir. At that point, a soldier's effectiveness can become seriously compromised by states of seemingly unbearable despair.

Sometimes, shrapnel from these issues can be carried in the wounds of unsuspecting warriors into the Medial Zone and, even momentarily, past the border into the Innermost Sanctuary of our Centers. And, even if it is quickly contained, it still can have an impact. With each new vanguard, the impact of this intrusion must be aggressively confronted with every resource and energy at our disposal until it ceases to threaten the Center's harmony.

If warrior scholars working toward the Center take a moment to reassess just how far they have come from their pre-ReAfrikanized, demoralized state, they will be able to compile an impressive collection of moralizing factors which have a demonstrated record of countering yurugu's physical and mental assault against our being. This collection of factors has proven quite effective in keeping despair, for all intents and purposes, at bay. These essentials include:

- a knowledge of self and a commitment to the study and practice of a righteous Afrikan philosophy of life (spiritual, mental and physical)
- a fully functional integration and assimilation into the conscious community,
- economic independence,
- the support of immediate or significant (sanguine or social) family members,
- an equally dedicated complement,[168]
- having and rearing children (biological and social),
- the highly visible presence of internal and external threats to the enemy and knowledge of frontline imperatives and

- the audacity and sense of accountability expressed by Jenoch and other Asafo.

All of these we find nestled comfortably at the Center nurturing those present and awaiting those yet to arrive.

Grounded

We are not an arrogant people. We do not aspire to rule or be masters of the Universe. We do not seek to supplant the Creator with a falsified, prevaricating science or manipulate Creation with childish notions of purpose and order.[169] As direct ascendants of the Creator and part of Creation, we understand that it is not necessary for us to aspire to an unnecessary, impossible power over others to feel secure in ourselves and see/have meaning in our existence.

We love this planet. We love the soil which birthed us, the waters which cleanse, the life which sustains us, the air which gives our nommo[170] power. We know we are but the caretakers of this immeasurable Creator-given, life-giving treasure. We do not own it.

When we are our natural selves, we feel the same for Asase Yaa[171] as we do our biological and social mothers. It is not in us to disrespect what sustains us and leads us in the path of divine wisdom. It is not our place or prerogative to misuse or abuse her. In every way imaginable, we are her offspring, her children.

So, it only makes sense for us to have always valued land and our communal presence on it. And, though we are not alone in this reverential attitude, every people does not share in this normal human posture toward that which we owe gratitude.

In fact, the lie has been circulating for quite a while now that Asase Yaa was held to be sacred in the traditions of all people. This is not so. And this offensive fabrication in the face of historical fact, designed to humanize sacrilege, must be understood as just another effort to euroversalize deep-seated abnormalities by attributing the rape, pillage and desecration of Mother Earth to humanity.

One people is responsible for the logic,[172] perfection and forced spread of this diseased mentality. *They*, Europeans, masterminded this cataclysmic devastation. And, without question, it is they who continue to most disproportionately profit from this careless, systematic exploitation long after others have been forced to become involved in this abomination. And, be not misled. What they did to take this land, they will continue to do to keep it.

Others caught up in this frenzy have little choice. Or, at least, they are led to conclude this because they see no other means of economic survival. No one else is more responsible for this blatant, reckless disrespect of Asase Yaa from its beginning than the european nation.

Just the historical record of wanton decimation of animal populations is an inarguable indictment of the innate anti-nature stance of Europeans. "Endangered species" have been created by only one people.[173] The words of Standing Bear of the Ogala Native Amerikan nation are but one testimony relaying what the Indigenous People witnessed of these zoophobic, [174] herbaphobic, [175] geophobic, [176] anthrophobic, [177] essentially biophobic [178] people's special brand of ruthless, unprovoked "death, destruction and domination" across this land:

> As yet I know of no species of plant, bird or animal that were exterminated until the coming of the white man. For some years after the buffalo disappeared there still remained huge herds of antelope, but the hunter's work was no sooner done in the destruction of the buffalo than his attention was attracted toward the deer... The white man considered natural animal life just as he did the natural man life upon this continent, as "pests." Plants which the Indian found beneficial were also "pests." There is no word in the Lakota vocabulary with the

English meaning of this word...[the Native American] was...kin to all living things and he gave to all creatures equal rights with himself. Everything of earth was loved and reverenced....[To the European] the worth and right to live were his, thus he heartlessly destroyed. Forests were mowed down, the buffalo exterminated, the beaver driven to extinction and his wonderfully constructed dams dynamited, allowing flood waters to wreak further havoc, and the very birds of the air silenced. Great grassy plains that sweetened the air have been upturned; springs, streams, and lakes that lived no longer ago than my boyhood have dried, and a whole people harassed to degradation and death. The white man has come to be the symbol of extinction for all things natural to this continent. Between him and the animal there is no rapport and they have learned to flee from his approach, for they cannot live on the same ground.

The damage they have done is immeasurable. But their denial and the projection of this reprehensible, unconscionable drive to abuse and discard the human cradle onto others goes far beyond the ugliness of that damage. Yurugu has no business pointing at anyone. They have no basis upon which to say "we" did anything against Asase Yaa. They have not thought, spoken or acted in the way of the Afrikans they now want to claim as ancestors so that they can continue their scramble uncontested. There is nothing Afrikan anywhere in them. More than 900 generations of practiced barbarity on the glacial Caucasus and centuries of imperialist strivings to so-called civilization has completely weaned them of anything remotely Afrikan. If anything from this dismal record is to be admitted, it is that we must free the land from them.

Let neither marxist socialist nor democratic capitalist theory convince you that there is some impersonal economic system driving them to do what otherwise they would not. It is they themselves – pure and simple. An economy is the invention of the people whose mind it was created to serve. It fits their cultural personality. We are but pawns, conspicuously consuming favored live-ins, but pawns nonetheless.

And it is because of how natural we were before this in our ourstorical relationship with Asase Yaa that it is so painful to watch so many Afrikans throwing trash on the ground as they drive or ride in vehicles, walk, stand at bus stops, kwk., especially when there is a trash container nearby. It is as if they feel that their decline to the ranks of irreverent polluters is an expression of their individuality and power over others. It is as if this is a right, a privilege of some deserved inheritance which compels them to arrogantly disrespect all that cannot (does not seem to) immediately retaliate against their abuses, including the very source of their life.

But my outrage is tempered by an understanding of the deep level of mentacide most of us wallow in that allows us to unthinkingly disrespect Asase Yaa in this way. We have forgotten the Ma'atian Oracles of old, telling us to not "pollute the earth." We no longer recognize our own mother.

Knowing who we are, though, and have always been with respect to Asase Yaa, we have to ask just how centered could any collective of Afrikans possibly be without, in some way, being directly located on the land? The answer, of course, is that we could not. So, the need to secure land to create safe, sacred places, wherever we are, where our Centers can breathe and be themselves, should always and forever be a top priority for every warrior scholar. Without a resource base, we can have no Centers, no sacred, protected spaces within which we can be whole, productive, creative, happy humans. The land question must remain central to our nationbuilding activities. For we know that "all power is from the land."[179]

Even so, we should not allow ourselves to become nearsightedly focused on our own little pieces of land. Our Motherland is the first and foremost priority. Strong people protect their motherland. It is their strength and greatest physical evidence of their peoplehood. The Afrikan continent is the "ancestral land" of our nation. It contains the physical remains (which includes the earth they return to) and spirit of our Ancestors. This is our power.

Therefore, a cornerstone of nationbuilding is seizing control of our original land from alien invaders and protecting that control. As we acquire the intellectual tools to build our nation, we must also look toward acquiring the land to do so. Wherever this acquisition begins, it culminates at home.

In our "new" beginnings, as healthy models of Afrikanity, we must move beyond simple survival. But, in order to live, we must first survive. Without land, and its protection, we can have no guarantee of that.

And, just looking at land from the angle of basic physical/nutritional survival, we can see how we have quickly forgotten that land was a major factor in our surviving the Great Depression intact. As then, if we are to survive the current, deepening capitalist catastrophe, it will be because of our conscious conservation and use of land. We should not have to be reminded that before and during the Great Depression, and for a short while thereafter, we were still intimately connected with the land. We lived on it, knew it and cultivated it. The direct connection between life and good food was understood. Credit did not sustain us. Our heads and hands did. And, if we today had that same grounded common sense, we would be quite aware that the machines we ride in, as well as the multitude of other glorified trinkets we play with, cannot be digested for nourishment.

It is no accident that all revolutionary leaders speak of the need for land. There is a reason why all of our publicized efforts at gaining large tracts of land have failed miserably. Enemies have serious psychosocial needs to keep us physically dependent, which strengthens our mental dependence on them. (They cannot be themselves without having us remain what they imagine us to be.) "There are other ways to kill a people or colonize them, but none is more certain than the denial or control of their food."[180]

Land is not only economic, though. It is political as well. People identify themselves based on the space they occupy, by the boundaries they establish which distinguish them from others and allow them to be themselves in the global presence of others. A people mark their territory.

Again, we come back to the point of physically being collected in Centers. Wherever we may be, without the possession of land identifiable as our own, we cannot truly exist in this form. Indeed, the Ethiopian proverb that "life is worthless without a home"[181] rings so true for many Afrikans, centered and uncentered.

Though inseparable from the above, if we truly understand the connection of Afrikan people to the soil, [182] we understand the need and curative properties of getting close to it. Contact with what empowers us helps keep us sure and grounded. [183]   Obviously, cultivating our connection with Asase Yaa in every way possible should be an unqualified priority, from birth, for all who reside within our Centers.

Immeasurable Evil

Afrikans often lose sight of the obvious. We do this for many reasons, but the most common are (1) our desire for peace at any cost, (2) the anxiety that often accompanies the fatigue that comes with fighting a seemingly never-ending battle while being bombarded with images of our ongoing destruction and/or (3) just the memory of how much we have individually worked to move our community in the direction of the Afrikan Way when considering how much farther we might have come if others, who are unwilling to even consider the possibility that something is inherently insane about this reality, had only not fought against us, not to speak of simply doing their fair share.

Still, we often forget the obvious reason why we must fight for Afrikan liberation on this planet. The obvious is Yurugu. The obvious is an asilic, cultural and social personality inimical to everything Afrikan, everything human, everything natural, everything of universal order. The obvious is the fact of an ever present, predatory global occupation by a people who cannot tolerate difference, especially a difference so distinct and alien to their being as that of the Afrikan.

The obvious is that it is not possible, given historical fact, for us to expect to live as an autonomous, independent, landed nation of people in the presence of european asilic arrogance. In order for this to happen they must fall. We have to break from this insanity or we are destroyed as a people. A population who want to be anyone's but their own ancestors is not a people.

Zombies do not make a people. negroes do not make a people. Lost souls do not make a people. Hyphenated Afrikans do not make a people. Mindless freaks in heat, ignorantly guided solely by other-imposed, unbridled physical and emotional appetites of super consumption do not make a people. Without rebelling, you cannot recover what you have lost all memory of in an anti-Afrikan place consciously working to keep who you are unknown to you.

That they must fall if we are to rise is no more a question than that of us having to have fallen in order for them to have risen. There is order in the Universe. Recovery requires that the pendulum swing in the other direction. And, most of us, even many warriors, are not prepared to accept the measure of that swing and what it calls us to do.

Given historical trends and the contemporary reality, in order for this to happen, in order for the Afrikan nation to rise, the world as we know it would have to die and be reborn anew. It follows, then, that Europeans must be removed from power over us.

This conclusion is not a debate among warriors. Only those in the community who cannot yet truly imagine a genuine liberation for Afrikan people, whose vision is limited to crumbs and a master's love, would find a need to "discuss this further."

Do not be mistaken. Do not let the confusion of eureason take you beyond the truth of where we are and what haunts this place. They say that "the greatest trick the devil ever pulled was convincing the world he didn't exist."[184] We should not be so easily fooled. There is evil here, immeasurable evil. And that evil has come to lay an absolute claim of domination on this world. There is a remarkable record of this. Like good, evil has ancestors, too.

Evil is rewarded in evil places. And, as the historical evidence and all around us today continue to demonstrate, european society is an evil social organization. Europeans have worked very hard to carve out a space where they can comfortably be their godforsaken selves. This is most evident in their repeated invasions of others' domains. In these barbaric atrocities, they have murdered or otherwise forced everyone in these places to submit to the white supremacist ideal. From incipient seed to the farthest branches, their evolution reveals an "evil genius" at work.

People use all forms of euphemisms to window dress "evil," a most apt term. But there is no more accurate description of yurugu's mind and way of thinking, speaking and doing. No matter what name we call it, what angle we look at, what position or how deeply we find ourselves entwined within its deadly coil, it all boils down to evil. We only stay confused or experience being repeatedly blindsided and shocked about the immorality and unethicalness of the order in the chaos about us when we forget that evil rewards evil. It promotes and sanctions it. Goodness is not part of the equation, except in service of evil ends. There are no mistakes, no inadvertent acts, no contradictions.

This is one of the fundamental truths about which we should never become confused. Within evil, in evil environments, evil triumphs. That is its domain. There it rules, regardless of the delusion of peace and love. In an evil place, evil people thrive. Evil is rewarded. Evil spirits congregate and coalesce. Those who do wrong prosper. The more wrong, the greater the prosperity. In evil places, good people are punished and sacrificed for the good of evil.

It is only in good places where good prevails. It is only

there that good people, with genuinely good hearts, are rewarded for their warmth and openness to those in need of their service and love.

This land, this space, this society, is not such a place. It is a sick, evil environment, contaminating everyone and everything in its path. And simply calling it illness is to grossly understate its horrendous, pandemic impact. As with its ancestral source, Old Europe,[185] this rife, ravenous evil spreads outwards from its polluted center outwards as a plague. It is plague.

We cannot build in this place without removing the contagion. For, as it is, it can only contaminate our physical, mental and spiritual space. The ground, the air, the water, the people are saturated. Good and evil cannot co-dominate the same space. One must rule. The other must retreat. Good cannot be rewarded in an evil society or that society will not remain evil. There is only a pretense that there really is a battle of good against evil in western society. There is nothing that can win here but evil.

To stop naysayers short, this is not a comparative statement of Afrikan versus european society. We do not need to defend our analysis to anyone. Time is the test. And this test has already shown european society to be endemically evil. Therefore, because this is a family discussion, we do not need to make evil sound like it is less than it is. We only need to look at european society, the premier historical example of an evil society by any and every measure. We need not compare them with others to see it for what it is. They are the proven masters of evil. Only in vanquished defense of their evil ways might we need to look elsewhere to find relatively insignificant examples of their thought and behavior so that they can feel more comfortable in our presence. Simply put, european society, in and of itself, can be described in no other way except evil. And it knows it is evil. It protects its evilness as a mother her child.

"People are consumed by evil because of keeping close

to it, but not because of keeping away from it."[186] People avoids evil by walking along the righteous path which leaves evil unable to penetrate their righteous armor. Good character defends a righteous person from the vagaries of evil. She or he walks above what is wrong and, therefore, has no need to fear it.   Like those who are true believers in the power, will and justice of the Creator, these individuals are blessed with a divine protection because they aspire to and achieve a godlike state. They know themselves, inside and out. They are at peace with their vision and mission. They are at our Center. On the other hand, "the bad people, people of evil character, are they who fear needlessly, and it is their sin that causes them needless fear."[187]

Ujamma

The economy is that social institution which unites members of society into a network of acquiring, distributing and consuming the goods and services necessary for their collective survival. Like any other institution, a people's economics is more than the collection, flow and concentration of material things. At heart, it is that social circulatory system of tested and trusted relationships which form an exchange nexus that effectively functions to make this process of give and take perform effortlessly to the benefit of all individuals involved.

For our Ancestors, economic activity was not a matter of conscious thought, per se. Exchanging goods and services was rather perfunctory. Giving and receiving was not only the basis of interpersonal activities, it was also what made society work. Reciprocity was a naturally occurring cohering part of our daily interaction/socializing.

The economic institution facilitated the continuous flow of goods and services between individuals. The currency was in the individuals and groups who made up society. The continuous accumulation of wealth/reserves judiciously spread among all involved was the social objective.

As Amos N. Wilson articulated so well, economics more than anything else, is a set of relationships among a people, a normal, unpretentious flow of communal appreciation, responsibility and expectation. [188] And it is this "set of relationships," this social glue, that facilitates the development and distribution of needed goods and service among them. Economics is the creation, cause and direction of what flows. What is exchanged in that social current is only incidental to this.

Currency, then, or what flows, may change in form from time to time. But the sense of community obligation that enables the functional movement of this flow should remain constant if it is to be beneficial to all involved. And it is the strength of the "sense of community obligation" which determines whether the economy benefits the participating community or not.

If the "sense" is weak, with individuals feeling a greater loyalty and nurturing stronger ties to another dominant, predatory community, then the benefit to the community will be weak to nonexistent. If it is strong then the community will prosper considerably. It's that simple.

Therefore, material prosperity, although useful, carries only a peripheral, utilitarian weight to Afrikan warrior scholars seriously focused on sustaining family and nationbuilding. It should never become an overwhelming appetite, compulsive obsession or neurotic preoccupation. [189]

Therefore, although recognizing its utility, particularly in this social reality, we know that money is not our primary objective, for money cannot, in and of itself, solve any of our real problems. It's not supposed to. Money doesn't think. And it has no intrinsic value.

Globally, for us, things have changed from the time when we were at our best societally, a situation manifest only in the world/reality we created. However, genoculturally/spiritually we are still at our best. We just have to melt away the dross of mentacide to see the gold of the Afrikan creative genius. It is to this which we must return if we are ever to again be solvent, financially or otherwise. Shackles of mis-identity, divided or completely mistaken loyalty and the weakness inherent in misdirected and unrecognized potential must be removed. How profound is the statement that "the ancestors were makers, creators [and t]he descendants were finders, consumers." [190]   Unquestionably, this is an accurate description of our economic transformation under european, arab and asian imperialism.

A sense of being family and the trust that accompanies that feeling is critical to the economic side of nationbuilding. Without it, economically, we are simply indulging in an exercise of futility. Whatever wealth we create will eventually be wrestled from our hands by those who have waited until we have amassed enough for them to feel compelled to appropriate it and who are aware of this fundamental flaw in the quality of our relationships.[191]

If our Centers are to survive economically, this organic sense of family must prevail. We must return to our economic source. The communalistic idea perfected by our Ancestors, where people receive their fair portion of what they need but without the selfishness characteristic of laziness, must be the only economic order operating between individuals.

Communalism is the Way of our Ancestors. It is not something we took lightly or participated in only occasionally or involuntarily. It is not something outdated, which fits a former time, instead it is used, but hidden from us, by others to pursue their organized, collective interests against us.

Inside our Centers today, this is how we should relate to each other. Outside of them, politico-economic relations are another matter. There is nothing in communalism which negates progress or, in a defended territory, cannot be practiced as it should among those in agreement that we are one people, one self-respecting loving family.

Communalism entails taking care of each other at the most personal of levels. In short, all community members willing and able to contribute to the whole must have all of their needs met. Reciprocity is the watchword. Communalism calls for a pooling of resources, to include time and energy.

Laziness is to be avoided at all costs because of its ruinous tendencies within communally organized social relations. This understanding bears fruit in the traditional Afrikan reality where there is a striking absence of laziness[192] and, especially, the "comfort corruption" found so heavily emphasized in the western privilege, leisure and pleasure oriented mind. In the West, laziness is seen by workers and "leadership" alike as a deserved perk of privileged positions.[193] And, though some Afrikans may possess more resources than others in the community, wealth is a group, not individual, function. Certainly, individual wealth can exist, but not in the presence of extreme poverty.[194]

The persistence of others' lies about, and our tradition of, communalism, cause many of us to question whether the individual is an extension of the community or if the community is an extension of the individual. For Afrikans, the answer is found in both. Although the community is the dominant center, individuality is a major force in personality development.[195] For the European, though, the answer lies exclusively in the second conclusion because the individual is the center of every concern.

Afrikans are genoculturally, spiritually and, therefore, psychologically connected as a people. The individual, though important beyond measure, is peripheral to this fact. Naysayers are in denial of this because they are confused about their origin and of the significance of origin and lineage in assessing the meaning of self. They are determined to make the Afrikan Way european.

Afrikan society is *familistic*. The family takes priority over the individual. But this must not be understood in the western definition of the preeminence of one thing negating or subordinating the other to the point of relative obscurity or an absence of power.

Indeed, there are many Akan proverbs which warn against individualism: "One person does not build a town." "One person alone does not arrest a lunatic." "One person alone easily becomes anxious." "The brother of a single person is money." "The head of a single person has no thoughts." "One person alone is a slave." "A single person is not a warrior." "I am because we are" is the most popular of these.

Marcus Mosiah Garvey also sagaciously illustrated the ourstorical continuity of this Afrikan priority of community when he proclaimed: "The ends you serve that are selfish will take you no further than you yourself, but the ends you serve that are for all, in common, will take you into eternity."

Afrikans understand the simplest, but most profound, lessons. For example, when people have good things done to them, they are encouraged to do good to others. When this is a naturally occurring phenomenon within a people's institutions, it does not have to be faked or forced. Goodness, in this respect, is socially cyclical in effect. A predominance of selfish individual acts within communities, on the other hand, generates selfishness.

Goodness is augmented by personal service between individuals. And one of the most telltale forms of personal service is bartering, which was a normal part of the economic way of our Ancestors. It logically follows, then, that it should be of ours. The trading of skill for skill, skill for material resource, material resource for finished product, finished product for services, or any combination thereof, must form the core of how we relate to one another within the Centers. Nothing within the economic institution builds trust and ensures independence better than bartering because it is a highly functional practice in the presence or absence of individual or group surplus. Furthermore, bartering makes exchanges personal, thereby serving as an organic social cement, whereas currency is a much more impersonal, mechanical form of exchange.

In the event of individual or group surplus, what the Nigerians call the "esusu," works well to communalize otherwise impersonal currency. In this economic practice, each member of a select group donates part of his or her earnings to a collective pot, which is regularly distributed to one of these members as a windfall to improve his or her condition.[196] It, too, involves and cultivates trust.

How we economically interact with those existing outside the Center should be determined by the history of our relationship with them and what, if anything, we *need* from them. Dependency on others for anything should be minimized at all costs.

Fihankra

When Afrikan men and women think as warriors, i.e., have no question that we are at war, they act as warriors. They become who they imagine themselves to be through visualizing themselves as already being that. It is not a matter of simply thinking (dreaming) of what they are capable of or want to become. Instead, it is thought manifest in conscious action that places them on a direct path toward a mastery of whatever qualities there are that they wish to perfect in themselves.

For warrior scholars on a mission of being models of community defense by actively engaging our enemies, the practice of preparedness is the most critical and enduring extension of that thinking. No doubt, sound security at home and effective martial tactics and strategies come as a direct product of practice (preparedness). In the end, warrior scholars must practice dynamic and proper security procedures to the point where they have been internalized and require little conscious thought. In other words, the dress rehearsals must continue until living defensively becomes second nature. Such an independent, highly disciplined approach to preparedness begins in the homes we sanctify and live in, the schools we build and teach and rear our priesthoods in, and the communities we progressively empower and ReAfrikanize through our own selfless, tireless effort.

How do we train ourselves and children to always operate as if the enemy is anywhere and everywhere poised to strike and, yet, live freely and happily at the same time? How do we make a defensive posture normal while stresslessly and calmly acting lovingly towards each other? What type of training would be required in making our children fully aware of the dangers of an insane, evil environment without making them reactively paranoid of everyone and everything around them? How do we stay on red alert without it harming ourselves or loved ones? How can we operate as warriors whose sacred space is the very epicenter of the military conflict, yet behave toward Afrikans within this space as if they are living in a fully "demilitarized zone."

It is not as difficult as it sounds. The latter issue, that of maintaining a peaceful sanity and a feeling of belonging among our children, is the easiest. Simply put, they need to know that they are loved. They need to feel that they are in the hands and command of adults who would willingly die for them, without second thought.

Having already been achieved in Afrikan homes, that is followed and augmented by the more difficult process of preparing for war. And this, like the responsible, disciplined demonstration of love, is also less difficult than one might imagine. All we need to do is add the sense of responsible precautionary common sense to all that we/they do.

Examples of implementing this in Afrikan spaces involve practices as simple as: (1) consistently checking for who is outside the door before opening it, be that the bathroom door, front and back door or car door, (2) learning to watch for shadowy movements behind and around plants, structures, vehicles and in relatively distanced places in the home, school and community center, and (3) taking the long way home and driving by lesser protected residences of others in the Center, just for the sake of it, or driving around the block one more time after leaving home to make sure that, that unknown individual or suspicious car has not become an active threat, and calling to report the suspicion to those left inside.

As our Ancestors, who studied the Universe as the macrocosm from which we should model our thought and behavior, we must find those "teachable moments" which genuinely allow us to demonstrate appropriate defensive tactics and strategies to our warriors-in-training. These occasions should also serve as opportunities for us to learn from, and reinforce these thoughts and behaviors, in ourselves.

In this respect, ants can be very instructive. If even a small hole is made in their hill (community abode), especially on warm, sunny days when they have brought their eggs near the surface for the warmth, they *immediately* come out, in force, searching for the destructive threat and effectively deal with it. There is no momentary pause while they contemplate or debate over what to do or the consequence of dealing with something, in some cases, obviously powerful enough, in one blow, to cause significant damage to their home. They instinctively act.[197] "Instincts" can be socialized into humans. We call these behaviors second nature.

And, even when there is an apparent fear of the threat in the animal kingdom, the safety of the children take priority over inaction. Not so long ago, a video of some water buffalo on the Continent was circulating on the internet under the subject title "Battle at Kruger."[198] One of their calves was captured by some lions intent on making a meal of it. At first, they continued on, distancing themselves from harm, seeing if the calf had the strength to escape of its own volition. But then to the lions' chagrin, after realizing that it could not free itself from their grasp, they returned to reclaim their own, using their horns and hoofs to attack the pride and even jettisoned a lion with a horn. The lions retreated and the water buffalo continued as before, liberated calf in tow. We should be so furious and spontaneously courageous as we complain about what others are doing to our children and families.

Vigilance about potential threats to the community is the prerogative of those who have decided that they have a special role in securing Afrikan premises. Sentries by choice, these mobile soldiers are aware of each other's presence and body language. And they spread themselves out enough when there is a gathering so that anything "odd" or "out of place" is easily detected, surrounded and removed as a threat without alarm to the other participants. Such conscious courage leads seasoned warrior scholars and those in training to automatically make sure that their vehicles are always parked with the side of the one most in need of defense facing the destination so their vulnerability is limited. They are always identifiable as those defenders who open the door and step out first to recognize and confront any external threat (a reverse of the showy nonsensical european chivalry of putting the female in front on defenseless display).

The same reconceptualization of what defense should be in the Afrikan community applies when a couple or family is coming around a blind corner. The same applies when climbing and descending, particularly stairs. At crucial, questionable or life-threatening times, a man placing himself before a woman does not constitute sexist thought or action. These calculated moves speak to the exact opposite quality. The protector should always be in the position to best break the other's fall. He or she who defends is always between the threat and the potential victim.

I do not believe that our Ancestors' everyday normative practice of this basic level of security is more evident than in this statement by Anthony Ephirim-Donkor.

> To underscore the protective nature of the paternal spirit the sleeping arrangement of the Akan is such that the male always sleeps in front of the female. The sleeping position must be such that if the woman has to get up she

may have to go over or around her husband. What is meant here is that the man not only protects the woman spiritually but physically as well. In times of danger the man is the first to rise up to confront whatever the perceived danger or threat is. He must have unimpeded access to the door to arrest the threat, and by the same token be the first to be attacked.[199]

Unlike the many eurocentric (especially feminist) misinterpretations of the functionality of gender roles within our traditions, this statement gives contextual respectability to the Akan proverb that "a woman lies behind her man."

It is always amazing to me the pride our young, male warriors-in-training take in inconspicuously following our Sisters who are leaving Afrikan functions to retrieve their vehicle parked nearby or at a distance. People should avoid leaving the premises of a fihankra [200] alone, especially our children, Sisters and Elders.

I am always proud when I see an elder leaving a function with security, whether that elder recognizes it as such or not. In fact, one of the most powerful examples of warriorhood I have seen is of an experienced Brother we know who, instead of coming into a lecture and partaking of the sumptuous meal afterward, sat outside in the shadows across the street and watched for potential threats to members of the community coming, going and milling around until the day's activities were basically over. He reminded me of the blacksmith in some Afrikan villages whose residence was beyond the communal social space, but who saw no disadvantage in the solitary job of minding the perimeter for threats against that sacred space. John Henrik Clarke spoke of the importance of instilling this level of discipline in our warriors-in-training when he said, "we should produce a caliber of young people who can take on the loneliness of struggle."[201]

These are but a few of the examples of the commonsensical security which should be evident throughout our community, every day, all day. Just like running one's family is practice for running one's nation, this preparedness is baseline for national defense.   All of these things, and whatever else any given situation dictates, must become reflex thoughts and actions for our warrior scholars in order for us to create an environment where we can naturally be ourselves without the stress of having to be, at the same time, security.

To some, this may sound oversimplified.   But not everyone is already a warrior *first*, making thoughts and actions of security second nature.   For many, this will be a trying and telling adjustment.   At first, this adjustment will be awkward, taking away some of the ease with which one goes through normal life in an Afrikan household, classroom, community or alien environment beyond their borders.   But practice will make the adjustment easier.

As a final point of note, warriors need to think in terms of a defensible position.   You cannot protect your community in an open field.   War must be studied, much more than it is. Without study, we cannot know our enemy.   If this is to be more than talk, i.e., a loud, protracted, meaningless, distractive conversation while the enemy continues its path of destruction throughout our community unhampered, then the art of war must be studied and rehearsed far beyond what it is now.[202]

The Role of Elders

Every day that dawns brings events from which the face is forced to turn. I speak out strongly against it. My limbs are heavy laden and my heart is heavy with grief. It is painful not to speak about it. Another heart might bend or break, but a strong heart in the midst of difficulties is an ally to its owner.

Khakheper-Ra-Soneb

As the Maafa progressively broke down our communities into their most fragmented dysfunctionalities, so too were age-based roles significantly destabilized. Though all groups within our community have been affected, the duties and obligations most deformed by this massive devastation of Afrikan culture and society have been those of our elders. And it is our Elders who sit at the heart of the protection, maintenance and intergenerational transference of our Way.

In our traditions, it is the purpose of the elders to bring and oversee the sustenance of order, along the lines of what has been passed on to them, in the community. It is to them and their great social and political responsibility, so vital to the empowerment and stability of the Center, to which we now turn.

In our effort to move as far away from european "conceptual incarceration" as possible, we have learned that naming ourselves is vital to this process. One of the terms that carries an extremely negative connotation is "mentor." It reflects a deeply-rooted homosexualizing agenda which is absolutely anti-Afrikan. [203] To confront this intentionally propagated misconception, elder warrior scholars encourage us to use the term "Jegna" when referring to those individuals who have seriously taken on the responsibility of leading us, their "Teumari,"[204] and especially our children, in the Afrikan Way.

One of these elders, Nana Kwaku Berko I-Ifagbemi Sangodare (aka Wade W. Nobles), has given us a resplendent definition of the Jegna which we will briefly look at in terms of its applicability to identifying the worthy characteristics of seasoned, senior warrior scholars. In the tradition of the Afrikans of Amharic ethnicity, he defines Jenoch (the plural of Jegna) as:

> those special people who have (1) been tested in struggle or battle, (2) demonstrated extraordinary and unusual fearlessness, (3) shown determination and courage in protecting her/his people, land and culture, (4) shown diligence and dedication to our people, (5) produced an exceptionally high quality of work, and (6) dedicated themselves to the protection, defense, nurturance and development of our young by advancing our people, place and culture.[205]

While the definition implies a degree of maturity and experience not usually exhibited by Asafo or those mature adults only beginning their Sankofan journey, it speaks to the complete state of being to which all our warriors should ceaselessly aspire.

Jegnahood implies eldership. It is a logical assumption, in a normal Afrikan society, that individuals will experience a progressive paralleling (and movement toward convergence) of aging and the mature handling of power and responsibility over the duration of their lives. And, because of this natural connection of age with maturity in the Afrikan mind, if we are to understand what a Jegna is, we must understand what an elder is. For, in our tradition, they are one in the same.

Elder (or Nana[206]), as an Afrikan designation, identifies persons of an advancing age in the community who have accumulated a vast working knowledge of their people's traditions (normalized, spiritually deduced, functional beliefs and behaviors). We could rephrase this to say that an elder is one who is learned, practiced and passionately committed to, the Way of our people. And, because of a lifetime of demonstrated commitment to these principles and practices, such worthy individuals are sought out for the active, dynamic wisdom that has maintained the traditional integrity of our families, community and nation in the face of the forces of time (change) and circumstance.

Elders are considered beyond reproach and held in the highest of esteem. They are conscious men and women of character who recognize their accountability to the community. They speak in a communal, not individual, voice. They know the value of quiet contemplation and listening, a valuable knowledge gained through life experience.

Among Afrikan people, Elders are greatly honored. Their reputations precede them. The evidence of their character is found in their lives full of Afrikan work. Their wisdom is highly valued, for Afrikans believe it an act of prudence to follow the wisdom of the wisest among us to keep us sane and together.

Ourstorically, Afrikans spend a lifetime in pursuit of a character deserving of the honor of eldership. Eldership, like ancestralship, is earned.

> Both knowledge and intelligence are developmental in nature, reaching full expression in individuals who mature to eldership. Yet age alone does not qualify one for attainment of this station. The person who does not exhibit mental maturity and acuity is excluded from the company of elders. The older person who lacks common sense is referred to as useless (*opanyin jyangen*) or foolish or stupid (*kwasiampanyin*).[207]

Some of our young today make this distinction using the

labels "Elder" and "older." Some Afrikans have chosen not to pursue eldership. They simply grow older and older while becoming less and less Afrikan, every year working more and more to move us away from the path of our Ancestor. In fact, as a result of our systematic cultural misorientation, subtle suicide and spiritual disconnect, increasing numbers of us seem to welcome this trap of treason against our Ancestors and, therefore, ourselves. Of them, we must be cautious, for nationbuilding is a people's effort. As in our tradition, an old fool without vision, who gains satisfaction in promoting a defeatist attitude among his or her progeny, should be dismissed for the treasonous simpleton he or she has spent a lifetime becoming.

However, many still know and actively embrace their mission of Afrikan liberation. It is these Elders who work to hone warriors for the frontlines of Afrikan sovereignty and sanity who should ever have our complete gratitude and attention. Such Elders have repeatedly proven their worth to our community. They have spent a lifetime acting in the interests of Afrikan people and, therefore, even though human, they should always be beyond reproach. The honor of speaking for us, of guiding us, of correcting us, moving us along the Afrikan Way, is justly theirs. Therefore, our Elders must be wise and articulate, for they explain our truth to us. We ever sit at their feet in anticipation.

An elder Sister once said to me that if Afrikan male elders would only act as warriors our young men would have no questions about what to do. Their duty would be crystal clear. Undoubtedly, this is true. However, it would be unfair not to include this wisdom when speaking of our female Elders, for we are also losing many of our daughters to their search for themselves within a eurocentric reality.

Our tradition, and what must obtain in our Centers, is one of responsible eldership. It is distinguished by an ourstory of uncountable senior men and women who did not see their lives as dedicated to and limited by an alienated, competitive obstacle course navigated in preparation for a leisurely, irresponsible, unaccountable retirement, before a final, lonely death. In the Afrikan tradition, becoming an elder has always been a highly valued goal in life, an honorable, deeply respected aspiration. It was and, within the conscious, centered community, remains a privilege bestowed only on those who have lived a righteous life full of the earnest and devoted fulfillment of a beneficial duty and obligation to the community.

Those, found incapable of fulfilling this social contract for reasons beyond their control, were/are forgiven. Those unwilling, for no sensible reason, were/are shunned, dismissed as cowards and/or traitors.

Our elders are held the most responsible for their thought and behavior, as well as the discipline of those for whom they are the guardians, because they are the most experienced in the ways of our people and universal truth. Their wisdom guides the community in the way of its traditions. Because of their status, privilege and role in maintaining the community's sanity, offenses by them are least tolerated. Any knowing crime by them should be punished more than the same for those who are younger. "If someone commits a crime, there is a great punishment. But if an elder commits a crime, then the punishment is even greater."[208]

They should act better because their life's energy has been dedicated to consciously manifesting and defending Ma'at as a natural way of life among our people. Those among us who have aged but who have consciously ushered forgetfulness and chaos into our space should not be remembered. There are no excuses for those who have gained a knowledge of right and wrong through the experience of time.

Simply aging does not qualify one for eldership. And Elders are not self-appointed. They become our guides upon the agreement and insistence of the community. In the same way as other appointments dictated by the rules and approval of the community, their selection as Elders lies in the hands of the people.

Generally speaking, the foremost responsibility of Elders is to maintain peace and order in our community. It is the duty of elders to seek out extant and potential problems/disturbances in the "force" of the Afrikan community. They sit at the center of our ReAfrikanization and nationbuilding process. That is why, "if you are going to purify the people, an elder is never absent."[209]

It is an accepted Afrism[210] that, "wherever there are elders, affairs go on well."[211] Without Elders there is no tradition, no communal direction, no social aspiration, no spiritual connection, no circle.

> The traditionalist in training is taught to recognize that all societies contain elements tending to disintegration: objects, ideas, customs, values, acts that if allowed to run their course would end up ripping apart the members of society one from the other, each from all. To all these elements we give the short name of chaos....We are also taught that every society contains the elements of attraction: people, groups, ideas, images, narratives, proverbs, values, customs, traditions tending to bring the members closer together. It is our habit to call these elements carriers of cohesion....Before the time when Arabs came smashing into us, before the Europeans invaded us, the work of traditionalists was to look for the elements of chaos, gather them and burn them. That was the small part of the work. The large part was to stay constantly on the lookout for the elements of cohesion the way the healer looks for medicine, to gather them, nurture them, strengthen them, and to infuse their essence into society, strengthening it....It was the work of memory to gather from the past and bring into today the images of all the beautiful things that united us then, pull us together now, and should hold us together in the future. Because this work required devotion with no vacation, it was no different from our way of life. Call its root remembrance. Remembrance of all our history, the entire flow of the narrative of all our people; not brute remembrance but remembrance guided by purpose, remembrance focused on cohesion, remembrance

working for creation.[212]

The traditionalists are our Elders. Their mission is to keep us together within the bounds of our Way, without compromise.

If there's nothing above them to see, people tend not to look up. So, there has to be a precedence in action, here and now, wherever our Jenoch are, for Teumari to witness which will motivate them to earnestly desire to fulfill their warrior's mission. Our Elders must set an example of warriorhood in the tradition of the ageless Afrikan warrior. It's time for a gathering of old men and women. It is time for a vanguard of Elders willing to forsake their fixed income and ignore their aches and pains to clear a revolutionary path by practical example. Acts of liberation can only be taught through demonstrations of liberation. "The old person who incurs debt, he says how much of it will he be around to pay?"[213] What is there to lose, but one's ancestralship?

The greatest heroes of a people are those who die for them in the ongoing battle for their freedom to choose and determine their children's life chances and vision. Warriors don't resign or retire. The concepts are foreign, ideologically speaking and realistically, to the tradition.

Age is supposed to bring wisdom, a greater working knowledge of one's mission. Age should become warriorhood, not be a barrier to its fulfillment. We see in our midst many worthy examples of those whose age is an asset to us because their lives exhibit the accumulated experience of warrioring and giving vision to the rest of us. Baba Hannibal Afrik, the Jegna to whom this book is dedicated, is a prime example of this personage. It is through the resilience of his practiced wisdom that we know that, in his own words, "when you fall, don't analyze where you have fallen; analyze where you stumbled." Unknown to those oblivious to our struggle for self-definition and self-determination, each one of these seasoned warrior scholars, these Jenoch, have done what the Ancestors could ask of a man or woman for our Way. They have been exemplary determined nationbuilders.

What we need is more loving elder Jenoch who do not aspire to retirement, who know that, for a people at war for their very sanity and existence, being a warrior is a vocation, a life's philosophy, not a hobby or game.   Those aspiring to a life of nationbuilding should study the work of our Jenoch and do what they do so that our tradition of honored eldership can be perpetuated.

142

<u>Conclusion</u>

You've got to be prepared to lose your life in order to gain your life.

Queen Mother Audley Moore

Being centered means actively thinking and living in the revolutionary consciousness and dynamic sacred space where the essence of what our Ancestors defined and lived as Afrikan people is at its purest and most densely concentrated. Centeredness is the highest level of ourstorical and visionary consciousness [214] giving an unqualified, complete sense of meaning and purpose to being Afrikan. It is a spiritual, mental and physical state of being. Without being centered, Afrikans are merely rotting pieces of driftwood floating directionlessly around in another's sea of insanity. Lest we forget, "a vagrant makes enslavement come."[215]

If we are to build an Afrikan nation in the presence of our enemies, then we must work toward establishing more reasonable, discriminating boundaries between ourselves and those who would destroy us. We have to build fortresses to protect those who are, and that which we define as ours. We have to construct and fortify impenetrable Centers. This is the mandate from our Ancestors.

If we recognize that two of our innate qualities as a people are a heartfelt sense of respect and openness toward people outside our nation and a "live and let live" [216] philosophy, which are equally two of our most suicidal faults in this predatory, anti-Afrikan reality, then we must reconfigure them so that they work for us both in relation to each other and in relation to others. We must truly go back and systematically study who this openness applies to and why it does not apply to others. We must focus our genius on helping every potential Afrikan return his or her energies toward the practical and ourstorically grounded application of these values/virtues. We can only again become empowered through the uncompromising reintroduction of our traditions in our community.

We need to have a vision of ourselves that is more than just that of being enduring and long suffering, regardless of how incredible our tolerance and resilience and the lessons this holds for humanity and those yet to come through us. I refuse to accept that this is the only possibility, that we must be the sacrificial lambs of european ascendancy. We are so much more than the asilically uprooted, hand-to-mouth survivors we see about us today.

Aspirations of returning to our source and recreating its physical magnanimity are fundamental to this reawakening. But, such aspirations must generate more than just the recognition that we are each other's genocultural connection. We must see ourselves as an army of one, aggressively, progressively, unrelentingly marching toward our return to power.

We are not on a march to be the best at getting along with people who have never known how to get along with anyone, including themselves, except to better position themselves to manipulate others more. We were not sent here to be the best at being someone else's children. And it is too far beneath us to elevate the saving of someone else's reality as our claim to fame. We are marching toward saving this world for us, for our Ancestors, our progeny, our Spirit, our definition of reality, from those who would, in their childish devilment, carelessly leave it in ruins.

We waste so much time and energy trying to convince enemies that any steps we take toward our liberation are safe for them, that our liberation is not a threat to their comfort or assumed supremacy. This strategy of polite pseudo-empowerment is laughable, and quite telling of our lack of self-esteem. Any movement toward a true, uncompromised Afrikan liberation automatically presents a clear and present danger to all imperialistic realities whose rule requires even a partial submission of Afrikan people to their will.

Therefore, to be Afrikan and victorious requires a warrior's vision. It is a vision of war that must remain unaltered until the full power of Afrikan people is again realized. This means that this vision must continue to invigorate our consciousnesses until enemies within can no longer be created by others and others no longer pose any meaningful threat to us as an Afrikan people. Otherwise, there is no victory, only an occasional, bloated pretense of power.

With this in mind, power must be defined appropriately.[217] We must know what we need and want independent of the interpretations and imperatives of alien minds. Otherwise, as history reveals, it becomes something less than what we need to become wholly free. For the same reason, we must clearly understand that influence is not power.[218]

Power is an act, an exertion. It is an informed and enforced decision. You decide to do and be who you are regardless of others' intentions to the contrary. Likewise, powerlessness is a decision. For any person under his or her own psychological volition, every decision to be or not be is a personal exercise in thought. This, no less so, applies at the community and national levels.

Power is the ability to have and fulfill an independently conceived vision. It is a precondition for being. You live it. You affirm it. Because our words are nommo, we naturally speak power into existence. We call it to amass within every fiber of our movement. It is what we must speak into existence if we are to have it in service to our liberation.

John Henrik Clarke spoke of how the Romans regularly greeted each other with affirmations of Kemet falling under their domination.[219] We, too, as our Ancestors who breathed words of genius into reality millennia before the ice forced Yurugu to retreat into the caves, must consistently affirm Afrikan liberation. At minimum, we must begin and end every encounter with each other with the greeting "Abibifahodie"[220] ("Afrikan Liberation!") or some expression, in the tongue of our Ancestors, that is equally powerful.

Power is the conscious, premeditated fulfillment of Afrikan life. It is absolutely evident in everything you do, in this reality and all others.

Power is a presence powerful people exude. It is felt like a force field full of spiritually supercharged energy stretching out in all directions from the mind and vision of those aware that they possess it. And those who possess it know that, in order to correct our predicament, we have to become a people who are much more concerned with our spiritual elevation than our physical satiation.

Power can neither be given nor taken, loaned nor borrowed, relinquished nor recovered. The threat of it can be extended to shield another, but that other does not possess that power. It does not change form or host, though it can be dormant in and/or forgotten by her or him.

Disingenuous, desperate, inherently barbaric oppressors will try to destroy powerful people from birth or, if possible, before their birth. That is why every scintilla of european time and energy has been devoted to the extermination of Afrikan people and consciousness, wherever we are found, no matter how disabled already. Nothing satisfies the eternally damned but the death of all else.

So, given this understanding, our circumstance and its obvious, only logical, resolution, how do we define victory? Do we modify it so that we can just subsist in this hostile world using the splinters of conspicuous consumption to fuel fires to warm our frigid extremities and wage sterile protests and rituals[221] to prop up our heads? Do we rush toward genocide so that our removal from Asase Yaa is quickened to reduce the pain? Or do we, in the strictest of confidence, organize and employ centered institutions until we have gained the momentum to separate, ReAfrikanize, empower and protect ourselves?

Those who appropriated all that is involved in our dignity must pay before it can be restored. "If a terrible epidemic descends on a town, it is confronted with a terrible medicine."[222] Never, before falling for the belief that we somehow had been miraculously transformed into the loved Europeans we imagine in our most vanquished dreams, was this ourstorical fact questioned. Never, before, have we forgiven the unforgivable. Never, before we became less than human in every meaningful way, was this possible. Only after our desperate yearning to sever ourselves from who we have always been, and become something not even the lowest life form would desire, did we become immeasurably less than our Ancestors. No matter what we have been told or wish to believe, there is only one way by which a blood debt can be repaid. Without question, this payment will be a key factor in our return to our traditional way of truth, justice, balance, order, harmony, righteousness and reciprocity.

Endnotes

1. Though this quote may appear to be written to Brothers only, as I indicated in the book from which it is taken, it is a definition that applies to Sisters equally. Whether we are speaking of the basic definition of self, what one needs to look for in a complement or the measurement of worker/leadership, this statement outlining warriorhood applies.

> [A]n Afrikan warrior scholar refuses to be at peace with anything less than the total liberation of his people. In fact, he should daily affirm that "I am an Afrikan warrior, a warrior scholar. I refuse to be at peace with anything less." He is culturally and politically a PanAfrikan nationalist. He believes that Afrikan people are Afrikans wherever we are found. I.e., the Afrikan warrior scholar believes that he should unselfishly employ the same dedication and energy to the defense and empowerment of Afrikans everywhere. The warrior scholar is not a racist. There is no confusion. His loyalty is conscious, race conscious, placing "Race First." Or, as the Honorable Marcus Mosiah Garvey would say, Afrikan warrior scholars are "Race Men." They know that to be pro-Black is not to be anti-white unless Europeans interfere with them doing their work. The Afrikan warrior scholar is an educator, not a teacher. He politically explains conditions so that his children, his students, will become better warrior scholars than he. Teachers only dispense another's information in order to train their students to become nonthinking citizens in an alien culture and society. The warrior scholar does not separate word from act. Leaving his people without a viable example to guide them in freeing their minds would be beneath his Afrikan reasoning. The Afrikan warrior scholar is a worker of the first order and, therefore, a leader by example. He is a doer, a nationbuilder, a maker of his people's way. In this respect, he is a nonintellectual in that he practically applies his knowledge. He does not see war waged in some debate, whether great or small. There must be a field application of tactics and strategies. As an educator, he fits information

into reality. He understands the cultural ourstory which has created his people's conditions and distorted their vision. He studies the problem, internally and externally, not those victimized by it. He does not define Afrikans as the core problem. And whatever internal symptoms he observes are logically attributed to our "cultural misorientation." He does not pass on his miseducation. He corrects it. He educates himself so that he can teach an ancient Afrikan truth. Therefore, he reads a revolutionary ourstory, the theory of causes and solutions to our people's problems. He feeds himself and the community from the library he builds. The Afrikan warrior scholar unconditionally respects Afrikan women. He is their defender, their lover, their divine complement. The Afrikan warrior scholar is an entrepreneur. He instills independence in other Afrikans by finding a way to provide, regardless of circumstance. He creatively controls the process of production, the input, throughput and output. He distinguishes wealth from income and power from influence. He pursues empowerment, not *sub*integration, because he knows that the quality of a substance is felt through its ability to autonomously determine its path. He creates meaningful employment, even if only because he knows that poverty spawns antagonism among a people. The Afrikan warrior scholar is a perimeter defender. He is the first line of defense for our people, for our most valuable resources, our elders, women and children. He is always prepared for any exigency. Afrikan warrior scholars are exacters of justice, using nonviolence as only one tactic in a collection of measures making up his strategic arsenal. He speaks to Europeans in their language. And he also speaks in the language of those Afrikans who mentacidally seek to help destroy our community. His words cut deep and clean. No one leaves with doubt as to his intent. He protects his daughters from misguided sons and sons from confused peers. He is ready to die for his children, biological and otherwise. (Mwalimu K. Bomani Baruti, *Asafo: A Warrior's Guide to Manhood*, Atlanta, GA: Akoben House, 2004, pp.vi-viii)

We must be clear that a warrior scholar is one who knows we are at war, studies history and ourstory, *and acts* on this knowledge.   Warrior scholarship, though, is not an intellectualizing pursuit. Though it has been promoted by some as the only way to true warrior scholarship, reading everything about us is not a prerequisite. Often, well-read individuals claiming to be warrior scholars do no more than read. Action is not part of their reactionary agenda.

Nonetheless, if we were to offer a required reading list which was requisite for access to the inner circle of warrior scholars, it would have to include Kwame Agyei Akoto's *Nationbuilding*, Ayi Kwei Armah's *Two Thousand Seasons*, Mwalimu K. Bomani Baruti's *Asafo: A Warrior's Guide to Manhood*, John Henrik Clarke's *Africans at the Crossroads*, Francis Cress Welsing's *The Isis Papers*, Erriel D. Roberson's *Reality Revolution*, Chancellor Williams' *The Destruction of Black Civilization*, Amos N. Wilson's *The Falsification of Afrikan Consciousness*, Carter G. Woodson's *The Miseducation of the Negro*, Bobby E. Wright's *The Psychopathic Racial Personality* and *The Autobiography of Malcolm X*. For further suggestions, see Baruti, *Asafo*, pp.91-96.

To logically take this point further, we should place a great amount of emphasis on the point that warrior scholars should not be elitists. Elitism is a stolen (appropriated), undeserved, arrogant sense of deserved privilege, maintained at the expense of others in the community. Elitists believe themselves superior. They believe themselves the only ones of their people or group capable of understanding the nature of problems and providing fitting solutions to them. They imagine themselves above the masses in intellect, "breeding" and the best qualified to know and speak truth. The self-serving subjectivity of their calculations notwithstanding, they see themselves as the talented tenth, five percent or whatever small fraction of the population they declare themselves to be. Mostly, in the circles of real exercised power in western society, their privilege is inherited, with no evident justification. Among the dispossessed, elitism, like colorism, is a "pathetic imitation" of the elitism Europeans practice among themselves and, as a people, against us.

For Afrikan people, elitism presents a very, very wrong order with very, very negative consequences. In our tradition, only humility deserves privilege. And that privilege does not come at the expense of others. It comes as a sacrifice by those given privilege who have earned the distinction of being obligated with greater duties and responsibilities to others because of it.

The presence of elitism (financial, intellectual, credential), however disguised in revolutionary organizations, is clear evidence of trends in them toward greater inequality, idle, counterrevolutionary chatter and arrogant, invidious hierarchical divides. It is evidence of control, without appearing to be so. If it were present at its inception, it was never a *revolutionary* organization. If it were not present at its inception, it is a ready sign of its impending decline as being a revolutionary organization because elitism signals political inertia for the masses.

We must be especially careful of intellectual (credential, esoterica) elitism, disguised behind cultural attire and disconnected, loquacious jargon. Interestingly, it is particularly prominent in grassroots organizations, in that the leadership manipulates their following by convincing them that they are fulfilling their will and not that of those in charge of the organizations. Such an intellectual elite

- base their authority and irreplaceability on mastery and control of esoterica (unexplained, and often unexplainable by the speaker, terminology conceptually "above" the membership, e.g., terms such as "scientific socialism," "hegemony" and "dialectical materialism").

- are elevated above the "masses" based on credentialism and expertise, even if not displayed as part of their public titles

- are skilled in the use of rhetoric and propaganda to manipulate and control the agenda and aspirations of the membership

- define organizational interests through in-group (clique) organization and coercion; although they claim egalitarianism and equality (usually propagating the idea that they are simply the appointed or anointed leaders of "peoples" organizations) of all voices, they systematically work to remove any dissenting voices that question the correctness and authority of their external or self-centered interests

- pursue the interests of external, more powerful interest groups such as feminists, marxists and homosexuals (external and infiltrated) as if they are their own (which, in some cases, they are)

- exhibit a greater tendency for cooptation, disguised as liberalism or alliance creation

- exist half inside, half outside the movement and, last but not least,

- are subject to the whim of the financial (usually alien) supporters of the organization who deal directly with them, usually without the knowledge or consultation of the membership.

Those in positions of power or influence acquired, maintained and validated through elitism will protect their privilege, and that of their children and others they may bring in, at any costs. Compromising the interests of the group becomes standard operating procedure in the effort to gain greater leverage over group members. Truth in procedure and decision-making must be made secret, something which works to lock the people out of an active participation in their future.

2. "Our Way" is the Afrikan Way which refers to the manner in which Afrikans have traditionally interpreted and acted in this world (before arab and european contamination). It is reflected in our evolved cultural imperatives and the spiritual, psychological and physical manifestations in which we naturally immerse ourselves. It is reflected in that common core of values, beliefs and practices that run through all Afrikan ethnic groups. (See Kwame Agyei and Akua Nson Akoto, *The Sankofa Movement: ReAfrikanization and the Reality of War*, Washington, DC:)yoko InfoCom Inc., 1999, Chukwunyere Kamalu, *Person, Divinity & Nature*, London: Karnak House, 1998, Maulana Karenga and Jacob Carruthers (eds.), *Kemet and the African Worldview*, Los Angeles, CA: University of Sankore Press, 1986, R. Sambuli Mosha, *The Heartbeat of Indigenous Africa*, NY: Garland Publishing, Inc., 2000 and Elleni Tedla's *Sankofa: African Thought and Education*, NY: Peter Lang, 1995.)

3. Eureason is the entire body of logic/reasoning that drives the european interpretation of reality into others' minds. It is the confusion that gives the illusion of a universal order to european thought and behavior. At the same time, for us, it is the Afrikan genius that, having accepted their thought as universal, determinedly seeks to rationalize the world as it has been organized by Europeans as normal for us based on this interpretation. It is the using of one's Afrikan genius to

rationalize the world from the european interpretation of reality. Succinctly, it is what makes Afrikans believe they are correct in willingly thinking and acting as if they are Europeans and act/react against anything, unapproved by Europeans, that is Afrikan.

4.   Europeanisms are those ways (thoughts and practices) of Europeans which travel with them throughout time.

5. References to the point and utility of "Black Firsts" have been made elsewhere.

> In our proud celebrations of "Black Firsts," we applaud Afrikans for *finally* repeating, or building on, the accomplishments already done by Europeans. We act as if we began here. While this criticism is not designed to negate any of our accomplishments while we have been dominated in this or any other land, it should force us to place them in the context of the accomplishments of, at the very minimum, 6245 years of advanced Afrikan civilization. (For those who would ask why I am counting today, we are still advanced. That is why they still seek to destroy us.)....Do not misunderstand this critique of "Black Firsts." We must be clear about what, in reality, we are doing to our children. Making our children focus on individually being "first" in an area where none of us has been allowed to go before in the European world is, on the surface, an honorable success-motivating strategy. It motivates them into higher levels of struggle. And it forces Black-into-white subintegration by using our children as battering rams to invade areas, heretofore in this white supremacist reality, inaccessible to us. But, at the same time, and an even more significant issue for Afrikan warrior scholars working toward ReAfrikanization and nationbuilding, our children's misguided infiltration, subintegration and, ultimately, assimilation and amalgamation into whiteness, becomes the ultimate goal of "Black Firsts" themselves. The goal becomes to show Europeans that we are as good as they in whatever they do and, therefore, in proving our equality in all things, they should feel compelled to welcome us into their hearts and minds with deracialized, open arms. This agenda for the success of our children is no more than the subtle subintegrationist strategy of a vanquished people trying to conceal their sacrificing of their own children's extraordinary talents to their masters, so they too can be accepted as human. No matter how you look at it historically, their goal is still to

convince Europeans, to influence them. Most of us still see them as holding all validating power that is socially and culturally derived. So our, and our children's, "Black Firsts," as measured against white progress, are designed to prove something to them, not us. (Baruti, *Asafo*, pp.85-86)

Of course, most of these anglo/europhiles are merely resting on the laurels of their glorified negro ancestors. They would never think to honor any Afrikan judged by western society as one who fought this racist system or who worked above and beyond the call of duty to move us away from an assimilated possession of european culture. The respect of negro historians is reserved for Europeans and those Afrikans who evinced some form of european validated success....The greatest collection of these historical figures fall into the category of "Black Firsts," epitomized by individuals such as Madame C.J. Walker, our first Black millionaire, who became rich by developing products to make our features look more European; or Crispus Attucks, who holds the distinction of being the first individual (Afrikan or otherwise) to lay down his life for the winning side in a european civil war that ended with the sovereign beginning of yet another racist european terrorist empire. negro scholars have to start and stop at piecemeal Afrikan "contributions" because any serious analysis of the lessons ourstory could bring us with respect to who we are as a unique cultural and traditional people, as well as the forms and outcomes of our interactions with others, might cause them to question the very foundation and reason for their false sense of security in the house of our enemy and be revealed for the intellectually impotent traitors that they are. (Mwalimu K. Bomani Baruti, *Notes Toward Higher Ideals in Afrikan Intellectual Liberation*, Atlanta, GA: Akoben House, 2006, pp.17-18)

6. There are two major intersecting politics of this pretentious "tolerance" now reaching widespread advocacy within european society.

And herein lies the contradiction of those Afrikan scholars who confuse themselves into believing that they are neoEuropeans, members of a colorless intellectual elite out to cleanse the world of blackness. In the same breath that these "intellectual mercenaries" argue that we must seek outsiders in order to learn to get along in a diverse world they emphatically cry that we have never been and can never unite because we are so diversified. If Afrikans are so different, with so much diversity among our own, as these negroes argue in their efforts to dramatize the impossibility of a united, PanAfrikan front, then why must we systematically go out of our way to seek others to experience diversity? From a global perspective, our motherland is the most diverse continent on the planet when it comes to resources, spiritual systems, complexion, language, family forms, economic conditions, kwk. We need not go even further and speak about the variety we find among Afrikans throughout our global Diaspora. Yet, the most vocal of these subintegrationists, assimilationists and interracialists feel that it is Afrikans who must be blended into Europeans and their allies in order to become whole. Even without the diversity we exhibit, these individuals still miss the point of who qualifies as natural members of the human community. It is the European, not the Afrikan, who has never learned to get along with anybody else. If anything, the Afrikan's hospitality and humility are legend and a fault relative to the European. Historically speaking, the Afrikan is the last who needs to learn to get along with others. (Baruti, *Asafo*, p.84)

7. Bobby E. Wright, one of our most insightful ancestors, in *The Psychopathic Racial Personality*, defined "mentacide" as a form of insanity that leaves many of us thinking out of the mind of the European as if it were our own. It is the state of being psychologically brain-dead and having one's thoughts replaced with alien ones, a state akin to being a zombie. "Mentacide" is derived from the root word *menta*, meaning "mental or thinking," and *cide*, meaning "to kill." "Mentacide" means to kill the mental process, to kill one's normal thought processes, essentially, to kill one's own mind. In that there is still a thought process at work, "mentacide" also means that an artificial, alien collection of thoughts and way of thinking have replaced what has been altogether suppressed or removed. (See Olomenji, "Mentacide, Genocide, and National Vision: The Crossroads for the Blacks of America (An Essay of Commentary)," in Daudi Ajani ya Azibo (ed.), *African Psychology in Historical Perspective and Related Commentary*, Trenton, NJ: Africa World Press, 1996, pp.71-82, Kwabena F. Ashanti, *Psychotechnology of Brainwashing*, Durham, NC: Tone Books, 1993 and Mwalimu K. Bomani Baruti, "Mentacide," in Mwalimu K. Bomani Baruti, *Mentacide and other essays*, Atlanta, GA: Akoben House, 2005, pp.5-10.)

8. For Afrikans, nationbuilding is the process by which our nation is rebuilt. Nationbuilding involves the social and cultural reorganization of Afrikan people globally toward the reconstruction of the spiritual, psychological and physical Afrikan nation. It is the process through which Afrikan people become sovereignly empowered as a politicized, self-defining and self-directing world people who consciously pursue their interests in the face of antagonistic others. The call of nationhood, and the conditions that brought us to this desperate point in the first place, requires that we accomplish this phenomenal collective feat with ourstorical remembrance, to the fullest extent of our capabilities as a people wherever we live on this planet without fear, apprehension or regret over the decision to be Afrikan.

9. There is a clear distinction between educators, teachers and programmers, something of which there is great confusion within the Afrikan community today. *Educators* are those who give knowledge and wisdom knowingly within an Afrikan centered context. Educators not only teach our children how to think but lead them to understand their power and the responsibility of that power to the Afrikan community. Self-interested, self-defining politics are at the heart of the instruction our educators give our children. *Teachers* are those who simply give information, although this information is inherently, eurocentrically politicized. Such individuals may even present the image of being Afrikan centered, but they are not. Yaa Asantewa Nzingha, one of our proven revolutionary educators, leaves no doubt as to the existence of this confusion in her statement "Reparations + Education = The Pass to Freedom" (in Raymond A. Winbush, *Should America Pay?*, NY: Amistad, 2003, pp.299-314). *Programmers* are the least of what our children need. These instructors do not even understand the vocation of teaching. These nonthinking individuals simply exchange income for spoon feeding us what they have memorized or reviewed overnight without analysis or consideration. They have no knowledge or concern, either way, for the needs of our children or nation.

10. Mwalimu K. Bomani Baruti, "Groundings with My Daughters," in Mwalimu K. Bomani Baruti, *Mentacide and other*

essays, Atlanta, GA: Akoben House, 2005, p.113.

11.   Mwalimu K. Bomani Baruti, Atlanta, GA: Akoben House, *Teaching Ourstory* (DVD), 2008.

12 .   ReAfrikanization is the process by which Afrikan consciousness is deliberately restored by Afrikans. It involves the unrelenting struggle to embrace an uncontaminated Sankofan return to our cultural roots. ReAfrikanization only comes about as the result of a serious, lifelong submersion into the study of our ancestral Way and our evolving, practical, applied rebirth within it.

13.   The asili is a culture's source.   It is the underlying principles and fundamental interpretation of reality in the Universe that guides its formation.   And it is the original, guiding imperatives that determine its unique characteristic personality of that culture wherever it finds itself.   It is the ideal model of thought and behavior that a culture, through its participants, aspires and continually works to become a perfectly balanced representation/reflection of itself.   As defined by Marimba Ani, who eloquently articulated this concept, the *asili* is

> ...the germinal principle of the being of a culture, its essence....[It] is like a template that carries within it the pattern or archetypical model for cultural development; we might say that it is the DNA of culture.   At the same time it embodies the "logic" of the culture.   The logic is an explanation of how it works, as well as, the principle of its development.   Our assumption then is that the *asili* generates systematic development....it is ideological in that it gives direction to development....Cultural *asili*(s) are not made to be changed. (*Yurugu: An African-Centered Critique of European Cultural Thought and Behavior*, Trenton, NJ: Africa World Press, 1994, p.12)

14.   Yurugu is another name for Caucasians or Europeans, as they have been exposed in the Dogon myth of Yurugu (Marimba Ani, *Yurugu: An African-Centered Critique of European Cultural Thought and Behavior*, Trenton, NJ: Africa World Press, 1994, Author's Note immediately following the Table of Contents).

Also known as the pale fox, Yurugu is a severed male spirit or principle. He is incomplete. His female half is absent because of a selfish and childish God-vying act. Because he was so determined not to wait for the Creator to finish creating him, he did not receive his female "side" before arrogantly completing himself. Therefore, it was lost forever and Yurugu will remain forever incomplete, destroying all in his path in an effort to find completion in the only way he knows how. This myth helps us understand the nature of the European as a function of a spiritual disconnectedness that is uncorrectable by us or them and, therefore, leaves us with a realistic base from which we can reasonably assess options for solving the problem of his blind, unrelenting destruction.

15. By "capacity," I do not mean "ability," as in the physical presence of the brain. I mean that such an individual is not so encumbered by eureason that she or he cannot even consider the possibility of an "alternative" (i.e., in this case, different and better) perspective. I mean that such an individual is intellectually curious and intrepid enough to openly listen to, logically consider, seriously embrace and permanently internalize correct Afrikan thought. Capacity here means mental, not biological, ability. In any case, warrior scholars must be very careful of using "alternative" as a descriptive of that which is Afrikan because it gives the impression that it is a lesser option and not the main thing we should be about, a mentality that keeps that which is European as primary and at our center.

16. Jenoch is the plural form of Jegna.

17 . A thought-provoking, "fictional" account of the nationbuilding possibility is presented in a work in progress by Rom Wills entitled *The Sankofans – An Afrikan-Centered Story*. The author conveys that its "main message is to create an Afrikan counterculture that is self-sustaining." It is visionary and, at the same time, very practical in terms of its possibilities. It can be found   at http://livinginblack.ning.com/profiles/blogs/2019163:BlogPost:2

3565.

18.   A useful sketch of the stages in this emotional journey home is found in the "To Become Afrikan" chapter of my *Asafo*, pp.163-171.

19.   We must also be careful when discussing culture and be sure not to confuse it with its less determinative customs. Custom is what is most visible because it is how a people acts out their culture. As such, it is the way things are typically done within a particular cultural context. It is that which is customary. Customs are forms of interaction and ways of doing things in relation to self and others that are internalized and practiced to the point of subconscious direction. They embody and define a people's daily routine. They are the habits that bind and define a people unto themselves. It is how they greet each other, arrange their day and night, show deference, barter, marry, give, receive, kwk. And, although custom is most commonly thought of in terms of actual practice or application, it is also why individuals as a people believe they should do these things in this or that particular way. While customs and traditions are not explicitly the same thing, they are inextricably intertwined and do not exist independent of each other. Traditions are the wider social/cultural context out of which, and within which, customs evolve. They are fundamentally, more deeply entrenched in a people's personality than customs, for they include that people's knowledge base, beliefs and customs. For example, tradition would be the way an ethnic group regularly comes together as one to unanimously decide important issues, while customs would be the way that the seating at such gatherings is arranged and what is the proper attire at such activities. Nonetheless, tradition and culture reinforce each other in meaningful (essential and critical) ways. Specifically, in relation to our discussion here, customs are expressions of culture and, therefore, much more susceptible to external influences/forces.

20.   This logic of this flawed "science" is explained in my essay "Evolutionary Science" thusly:

The idea of human evolution, as a cornerstone of european science, began in traditional european society as they began to rise out of their inherent intellectual and economic morass through robbing other people of their original thought and resources. Europeans appropriated science and developed it as a rational weapon for asserting that their aggressions against others were correct, responsible and, indeed, necessary for the "civilizing" (i.e., europeanization) of others. As they moved out of raw physical barbarism, they needed objective tools to prove that their way of organizing society, technology, work and possessions was superior to all others. And science provided those tools....That said, since they could not prove that any of humanity originated in Europe, they needed to overcompensate for this glaring discrepancy by proving that their late arrival on the evolutionary ladder was evidence of their natural superiority. A claim to an inherent superiority was necessary in order to justify their arrogance. Evolutionary theory did this by making the last first and the first last. And, in doing so, it made their violently aggressive thought and behavior tantamount to forward progress. Because, according to european evolutionary theory, the last to arrive is the best qualified to lead. And they were the absolute last and the most violently aggressive. Progress, or any change, defines quality in western evolutionary theories. The latest or newest thing, idea or being is naturally assumed to be superior to all that came before unless proven otherwise. (Mwalimu K. Bomani Baruti, *Eureason: An Afrikan Centered Critique of Eurocentric Social Science*, Atlanta, GA: Akoben House, 2006, pp.55-56)

21. Despiritualized means to be without spiritual content or essence in terms of the manifestation of reality and the interaction within and among individuals, groups, organizations and institutions.

22. An interesting glimpse inside the machine which controls and markets wants/needs to their and our children is seen in *Frontline*'s "The Merchants of Cool."

23. In *Why Are We So Blest?*, Ayi Kwei Armah gives an Afrikan centered interpretation to the substance of the Afrikan-European knowledge dichotomy as when knowledge and its acquisition are defined in European terms. He correctly observes that:

The search for knowledge should not be synonymous with increasing alienation and loneliness. In our particular circumstances it is so. It has been planned that way. Knowledge about the world we live in is the property of the alien because the alien has conquered us. The thirst for knowledge therefore becomes perverted into the desire for getting close to the alien, getting out of the self. Result: loneliness as a way of life. This loneliness is an inevitable part of the assimilationist African's life within the imperial structure. Because of the way information is distributed in the total structure – high information in the center, low information on the peripheries – overall clarity is potentially possible only from the central heights. The structures in the peripheral areas are meant to dispense low, negative or mystificatory information. The choices are clear. Those who stay in the peripheral areas intellectually, emotionally, psychologically, totally, are not lonely. They are in touch with home, not cut off. The price they pay for not being lonely, however, is that they suffer the crudest forms of manipulation, mystification, planned ignorance. Those who shift from the periphery to the center can hope to escape some of these cruder forms of manipulation. But the price they pay is loneliness, separation from home, the constant necessity to adjust to what is alien, eccentric to the self. All this is in the present structuring of the machinery for acquiring knowledge, not in the essential nature of the learning process itself. (London: Heinemann, 1974, *pp.32-33*)

This statement is briefly summarized in the table below which speaks to the intellectual, psychological and emotional state of Afrikans with respect to their location relative to european validation and subsidization.

CENTER	PERIPHERY
European	Afrikan
Alien[ated]	Familiar

Lonely	Together
Information	Ignorance (planned)
Positive	Negative
Subassimilated	Isolated
Manipulated (kindly)	Manipulated (crudely)
Cut Off	In Touch

Afrikans recruited into the "center" of european life and culture have eurosupremacy as their ultimate reference point, are aliens (i.e., alienated from their Afrikan selves, usually by themselves as well as Europeans), are lonely in a highly individualized fashion, have access to more information about the world and the dominant group's standard, "scientific" interpretation of reality, are perceived as being positively impacted in life, are subassimilated into the dominant culture and society, are benevolently manipulated by those in power and around them who disdainfully see them as naive children and are cut off from that which naturally gives them power and identity. Afrikans on the periphery of european acceptance and validation have that which is Afrikan as their center, live in an environment among people with whom they are familiar in life-affirming and life-giving ways, are part of a thoroughly integrated social/cultural community, are victims of a planned ignorance regarding the part of the known information about the world as defined by Europeans, are perceived in negative terms and are taught to see themselves accordingly, are isolated from the knowledge base of the dominant society, are manipulated viciously but are whole, being in touch with their people and selves. For those trying to make sense of Yurugu's constantly malevolent intent toward Afrikan people, and the relationship of this attitude relative to our disadvantage in their reality, whether we are in their center or periphery, it can be helpful to give thought to the Yoruba proverb "If one's head has a pot and one gave it to an enemy to inspect, he would say it was irretrievably broken."

24.   An Afrikan centered, working definition of civilization must be greater than the sterile one we accepted in our westernized state of mind.

> ...we must employ the knowledge of our children's treatment in our definition of civilization. The state of civilization should not be measured by the amount or level of mechanical technology a society produces or accumulates. It has been said that whether a society is a civilization or not must be judged by the quality of the life of its women. This should be changed to "its children." We say children because they are the most defenseless of all and dependent on adults for their well-being. The quality of their lives speaks to the character of the society developed by their parents. Therefore, using this definition, if significant numbers of a society's children are starving, homeless, mis- and diseducated, sexually violated, drugged or otherwise intoxicated, obese, suicidal, incarcerated and on death row, then that is not a true civilization. Obviously, people in love with the West who believe it is civilized are using the wrong indicators for measuring civilization. (Mwalimu K. Bomani Baruti, *Nyansasem: A Calendar of Revolutionary Daily Thoughts*, Atlanta, GA: Akoben House, 2008, Ahinime 31 | October 31)

25.   Though in mainstreamed terms, E. Franklin Frazier very simply answers the question of what distinguishes integration from assimilation.

> How does integration differ from assimilation? Assimilation involves, of course, integration for it is difficult to see how any people or group can become assimilated without being integrated into the economic and social organization of a country....But assimilation involves integration into the most intimate phases of the organized social life of a country. As a consequence, assimilation leads to complete identification with the people and culture of the community in which the social heritages of different people become merged or fused. ("The Failure of the Negro

Intellectual" in Joyce A. Ladner (ed.), *The Death of White Sociology*, Baltimore, MD: Black Classic Press, 1998 (first published in 1973), p.54)

Bearing that critical difference in mind, we can understand a more fractured subassimilation through the following definition of subintegration. Most Afrikans in western society assume that integration is a two-way process of equal "give and take." After all our hard lessons, the "melting pot" delusion is still alive and well in our community. Too many of us also assume that so-called integration is a positive and something to which we should aspire. However, integration is not what has happened. What Afrikans and Afrikan ideas and things that Europeans have allowed to be absorbed into their culture have assumed a lesser or subordinate importance and status, or at least have been given the impression of such. Therefore, in using the word integration, we may be using the correct dictionary denotation, but it is the incorrect connotation for Afrikans in the western reality. That being the case, we need a term that more appropriately fits this reality. *Sub*integration includes not only the basic ideal definition of integration but also the way in which Afrikans (and those ways and things Afrikan) are introduced and incorporated into (and recognized by) western culture and society. Be mindful that we are not here speaking of those ancient and traditional Afrikan ideas and things that were stolen and distorted into the foundations of european thought and behavior because those Afrikanisms are not accepted or admitted as Afrikan within european culture, thought or society.

26. Amos N. Wilson spoke well of the value of nationalism in an essay dealing with Marcus M. Garvey (*Afrikan-Centered Consciousness Versus The New World Order*, Brooklyn, NY: Afrikan World InfoSystems, 1999, esp. pp.66-80). Both he and John Henrik Clarke spoke to the problem of nationalism only being one of white racism. Clarke said that

> ...nationalism in itself is not bad. And it is part of the life of every people – and should be. But what makes the nationalism of Europeans, of white people, so different and so dangerous? Racism. The addition of racism added to

nationalism. Love of nation is nothing that one needs to look down on. It is something that can be respected in every man, in every nation. It is universal. But what we need to recognize, in dealing with white nationalism is that the ingredient of racism was added to nationalism, and this made it dangerous because it assumed that one people had preference over another people to the point where their gods told them to take away from another people anything they needed from that other people. (*Notes for an African World Revolution: Africans at the Crossroads*, Trenton, NJ: Africa World Press, 1991, p.252.)

Like so many other positive, people-saving terms we have chosen to run from in fear or disgust because of the historical use of them by Europeans against us, terms like genetics, segregation, radical, revolutionary and Afrikan (compromised into virtual oblivion by the hyphenated African-American), kwk., nationalism is only negative because of its use by Europeans against us. We should recognize that the reason Europeans and their negro watchdogs negatively define nationalism is that they know that its genuine acceptance among us would lead us to realize its unifying force and cause us to act as a people against those whose privilege is bound in their exploitation and destruction of us.

27. *Nationbuilding: Theory & Practice in Afrikan Centered Education*, Washington, DC: Pan Afrikan World Institute, 1992, pp.22-23.

28. A great amount of work has been done in this area by Kwesi Ra Nehem Ptah Akhan. His works can be found at www.odwirafo.com.

29. See Kwame Agyei and Akua Nson Akoto, *The Sankofa Movement: ReAfrikanization and the Reality of War*, Washington, DC:)yoko InfoCom Inc., 1999, Chukwunyere Kamalu, *Person, Divinity & Nature*, London: Karnak House, 1998, Maulana Karenga and Jacob Carruthers (eds.), *Kemet and the African Worldview*, Los Angeles, CA: University of Sankore Press, 1986, R. Sambuli Mosha, *The Heartbeat of Indigenous Africa*, NY: Garland Publishing, Inc., 2000 and Elleni Tedla's *Sankofa: African Thought and Education*, NY: Peter Lang, 1995.

30.   For those of us who can see beyond the eurocentric, it is only logical that no conscious, studious people could have existed for thousands of years without conceptualizing themselves socially. It is because of this commonsensical fact that we know that sociology, as a practical, thinking, functional discipline, comes into existence with a people's awareness of self. The awareness of self creates a social consciousness which, in turn, causes that people to interpret the what and why of their interaction. Written or oral, sociology is fundamentally inherent in any group who analyzes self for purposes of self-definition and self-improvement as one. We must use this and other scientific concepts, conceptually incarcerated and limited by european, supremacist *political science* (science as dictated by a specific people's political interests – see Mwalimu K. Bomani Baruti, *The Sex Imperative*, Atlanta: Akoben House, 2002, pp.49-50) to help us realize our responsibility for reconceptualizing every term significant to our social, cultural and spiritual being as Afrikan people so that these terms beneficially and truthfully apply to us as they do and have since our intellectual origins.

31.   Those within often project their divisiveness on us, claiming that being Afrikan, without also being European, is the disease, the imbalance. In their entrenched, highly politicized mentacide, they accuse us of atomizing the Race along "unimportant" lines. But, it is they who are divisive in bringing and harboring the alien Way in our midst and then pointing at us as faulty for rejecting it.

32.   Kwabena F. Ashanti, private conversation.

33.   Sankofa is one of the many Adinkra symbols of the Akan people of West Afrika. It literally means "go back and fetch it." The Sankofa symbol, drawn as a bird with its head turned toward what is behind it, is designed to remind us that we have to investigate and understand our past in order to correctly interpret the present. With this wisdom we can then make determinations as to which direction we should move in the future so that we will be guided toward our traditional ways of thinking and doing.

34.   ...*Kebuka* (pronounced kay-boo-kah), is a Kikongo word

meaning, in simplest terms, "remember." It is to say that we must struggle to remember the most deeply hidden intricacies of what we have been made to lose and use that memory to rebuild our future in line with those ancestral traditions. Baba Kimbwandende Kia Bunseki Fu-Kiau, who is my primary source for understanding this concept, has defined it as to "look back both physically, (with your eyes) and mentally with your mind; to draw from the past experience (both positive and negative); to rely on one's ground; [and] to link the past to the present reality before dreaming for tomorrow." He says that kebuka "is both a physical or material and spiritual word" and indicates that "Kebuka is the equivalent of Sankofa" in Kikongo. He states, however, that "...kebuka as a verb is more powerful and more active and has more regenerating power itself than Sankofa." Of course, with respect to the concept Sankofa, we know that there is no competition between Afrikan languages. All Afrikan tongues are rich. And the more words we have that speak to the necessity of remembrance to our contemporary sanity the better we are spiritually, intellectually, emotionally and physically able to engage our past, present and future as empowered Afrikans. Kebuka is simply a choice reflecting the need to have an additive Afrikan voice in the repertoire we use to speak a reAfrikanized reality into our nationbuilding efforts. (Mwalimu K. Bomani Baruti, *Kebuka!: Remembering the Middle Passage Through the Eyes of Our Ancestors*, Atlanta, GA: Akoben House, 2005, p.5)

35. By conceptual incarceration, we speak of a people's ability to think being circumscribed by

> ...a set of predetermined "concepts" and definitions to utilize in the "process of knowing". The alien or incorrect concepts themselves, however, inhibit the process of knowing and the knower becomes a prisoner of these alien "ideas". (Wade N. Nobles, *African Psychology: Toward Its Reclamation, Reascension & Revitalization*, Oakland, CA: Black Family Institute, 1986, p.19)

36. "Political Paths" in Mwalimu K. Bomani Baruti, *Notes Toward Higher Ideals in Afrikan Intellectual Liberation*, Atlanta, GA: Akoben House, 2006, esp. pp.111-122.

37. "Racism, Colorism and Power" in Larry D. Crawford

(Mwalimu A. Bomani Baruti), *negroes and other essays*, Atlanta, GA: Akoben House, 2000, pp.115-142.

38.   New Europe is simply those colonies that expanded out of Europe through invasion and theft of other peoples' lands, which evolved into separate geographical countries but which remain culturally European. Canada, Azania (South Africa), Australia, Israel and this country are prime examples of this. Old Europe is their point of origin, their fatherland. Countries such as England, France, Spain, Portugal and Germany are some of these originating countries. The difference between Old and New European countries is no more than one of location and age. Old and New European countries form one european nation. Their cultural core, their asili, is one and the same. (See "The Cultural Continuum" in Larry D. Crawford (Mwalimu A. Bomani Baruti), *negroes and other essays*, Atlanta, GA: Akoben House, 2000, esp. pp.41-42 and the essay on Kwame Ture.)

39.   Exceptions obtained but they did not deviate in Afrikan conserving, inclusive, natural intent.

40.   Kimbwandende Kia Bunseki Fu-Kiau's discussion of the "Vee" is pertinent here. In his explanation of righteous human development within the life cycle, as understood by our Ancestors, the closeness of ones spirit, mind and body to the Afrikan center as one travels this circular journey through birth, life, growth, death, spiritual ascension and return through birth reflects a person's power as a thinking, acting human being. Like the center of the circle of light made by the turning lamp of a lighthouse's beacon, the closer one is to the lamp, the brighter and warmer is the effect of the light. Though this is an oversimplified example, what Fu-Kiau calls the "Vee" is the light beam emanating from the lamp, the fan of light, from its starting point to the extent of its spread. The center remains constant. The beam revolves. This moving "Vee" marks the range of possibilities in terms of the nearness or farness one stands in relation to the Ancestral center as one moves through life. As Fu-Kiau notes,

> [T]he Vee in reality, is a living pyramid in constant motion, which follows the path of life....The closer one is to the center...the healthier and more powerful one is. On the contrary, the more distant one is from this center, the weaker and less powerful one becomes. (*Tying the Spiritual Knot: African Cosmology of the Bântu-Kôngo: Principles of Life & Living*, Brooklyn, NY: Athelia Henrietta Press, 1980, p.132)

What's most important for our purposes in this cosmological explanation is that the possibilities from strength to weakness, from knowing to alienation, from peace to chaos, range from the center to the perimeter. In this book's model, we have simply divided this range into three concentric layers.

41. See Baruti, *Asafo*, pp.157-158 and Baruti, *Nyansasem*, Osanaa 18 | August 18. Ayi Kwei Armah explains this naturally layered form of protection in *Osiris Rising* (Popenguine, West Africa, 1995, p.251).

42. We call what exists outside these Centers, and which fully surrounds them chaos, not because there is no order there for those who are not us. Their mind is an ordered chaos, very complex in its ability to stabilize incongruent and contradictory elements together. What they are, they build. We call it chaos because, historically, all who have sought closeness to us have been ill-intentioned. And, for an Afrikan to become involved in this anti-Afrikan chaos is highly destructive to the natural order of the Afrikan personality.

43. This does not contradict the point that Spirit vibrates at a higher and higher rate in the obverse direction.

44. For those wanting to theoretically question this model, the laws of physics may not appear to apply here because Spirit may seem to be limited to the vastness which lies beyond the outermost surface of the center complex. And, if this is the case, how could Spirit "feed" the innermost sphere without penetrating the middle and exterior layers? However, for thinking Afrikans, this ostensible dilemma is not a contradictory proposition. Fundamental to any scientific analysis investigated within Afrikan

minds is the understanding that Spirit is everywhere. That it is all pervasive is a given. There is no space it does not occupy. So, accepting that everything is of Spirit, and that these concentric spheres exist in the reality of the Universe, they are of Spirit also. The only serious thought which requires deeper consideration here is the differential concentration of different aspects of Spirit within the various layers of this Center. Those values which are disproportionately found in the Afrikan asili are more so concentrated in the Afrikan center than those more valued by other minds. It is not a matter of differential density, for each people has its Centers, only one of asilic selectivity. And this selectivity is more evident the closer we move to the core of the Centers.

45. It is imperative that we distinguish between feminism, a european tradition, from womanism and motherism, both Afrikan traditions. As I stated in *Complementarity: Thoughts for Afrikan Warrior Couples,*

> Afrikan women are womenist while European women are feminist. "Womanism" centers around working toward equality with and respect by men. It also holds motherhood as its most central priority. This must be contrasted with "feminism," which is simply the normal dominative psychology of Europeans, only concentrated in and directed by female politics. It is a european-style matriarchy without any true concern for motherhood or nurturance. Individualism naturally dominates this political orientation. We must recognize that spiritually barren women (whether married or not) spawn bastard, sterile, unemotional (even if loud and active) offspring. (Atlanta, GA: Akoben House, 2004, p.93. Also see Mwalimu K. Bomani Baruti, *Homosexuality and the Effeminization of Afrikan Males*, Atlanta, GA: Akoben House, 2003, pp.43-48)

46. Homosexualized, versus homosexual, is the more appropriate term for what has been happening to Afrikans who have become gender confused.

> Simply defined, homosexual*ization* is the process of turning individuals who would normally be heterosexual into practitioners and advocates of sexual aberration. Obviously, in order for this process to begin, there must be an original

homosexual group and one that is, from their beginning, not. Herein, when we are speaking of Afrikans practicing homosexuality, we are talking about those individuals who have been homosexualized, whether we say homosexualized or simply homosexual. (Mwalimu K. Bomani Baruti, *Yurugu's Eunuchs*, Atlanta, GA: Akoben House, 2009, p.7)

47. Akan proverb.

48. Ayi Kwei Armah, *KMT*, Popenguine, Senegal: Per Ankh, 2002, p.257-275.   Also see Baruti, Eureason, pp.10-11.

49. Akan proverb.

50. Mari Evans makes the clear distinction between rearing and raising our children.

> Raising can be satisfied by providing the essentials: food, shelter, clothing and reasonable care.   "Rearing" is a carefully thought out process.   Rearing begins with a goal and is supported by a clear view of what are facts and what is truth (and the two are not necessarily synonymous).   Rearing is complex and requires sacrifice and dedication.   It is an ongoing process of preparation. ("The Relationship of Childrearing Practices to Chaos and Change in the African American Family," in Carlos Moore, Tanya R. Sanders and Shawna Moore (eds.), *African Presence in the Americas*, Trenton, NJ: Africa World Press, 1995, p.306)

Mwalimu J. Shujaa speaks to this critical distinction in the academic setting in terms of "schooling" versus "education."

> I believe that for Africans in the United States (and elsewhere, for that matter) education must be recognized as a process that should reflect our own interests as a cultural nation and be grounded in our cultural history.   It should be a process of identity development within the context of Pan-African kinship and heritage.   Education is our means of providing for the inter-generational transmission of values, beliefs, traditions, customs, rituals and sensibilities along with the knowledge of why these things must be sustained.   Through education we learn how to determine what is in our interests, distinguish our interests from those of others, and recognize when our interests are consistent and inconsistent with those

of others. Education prepares us to accept the staff of cultural leadership from the generation that preceded ours, build upon our inheritance and make ready the generation that will follow us....The schooling process is designed to provide an ample supply of people who are loyal to the nation-state and who have learned the skills needed to perform the work that is necessary to maintain the dominance of the European-American elite in its social order. ("Education and Schooling: You Can Have One Without the Other," in Mwalimu J. Shujaa *Too Much Schooling, Too Little Education*, Trenton, NJ: Africa World Press, 1994, pp.9-10)

Schooling is a process *intended* to perpetuate and maintain the society's existing power relations and the institutional structures that support those arrangements....Education, in contrast to schooling, is the process of transmitting from one generation to the next knowledge of the values, aesthetics, spiritual beliefs, and all things that give a particular cultural orientation its uniqueness. Every cultural group must provide for this transmission process or it will cease to exist. (Ibid, p.15)

And I argue that this distinction is also manifest in those responsible for imparting knowledge in the classroom.

Depending on the setting, there are three basic types of individuals who formally instruct our children. The least of these are *programmers*. They do not understand the vocation of teaching at all. They are merely nonthinking individuals who receive income in exchange for spoon feeding our children what they have memorized or reviewed overnight without analysis or consideration (or, in most cases, even knowing) of the needs of our students or nation. Next are *teachers*. Teachers give eurocentric information also. Yet, much more so than programmers, they are consciously intent in their efforts to assimilate and subintegrate Afrikan children into european culture and society. And then there are our *educators*. These are those individuals who give knowledge and wisdom knowingly within an Afrikan centered heart and context. Educators are fully politicized nationbuilders, giving our children everything they might need to rebuild the Afrikan nation. In short, as Lerone Bennett, Jr. once wrote that "an educator in a state of oppression is either a revolutionary or himself an oppressor." (Mwalimu K. Bomani Baruti, *Nyansasem: A Calendar of Revolutionary Daily Thoughts*, Atlanta, GA: Akoben House,

51. "Miseducation" is a term coined by Carter G. Woodson in his classic book *The Miseducation of the Negro*, "miseducation" names that learning which is irrelevant to one's empowerment. It means to be wrongly educated. In his book, Woodson explains how Afrikans in colleges and universities are being taught subjects, theories, agendas and philosophies that are irrelevant to the elevation of Afrikan people, but which makes them feel as if they are being highly educated because this is what european academia say defines the intelligent citizen and is critical for the continued development of their thinking and leadership skills. He points out that a miseducation leads the student and graduate everywhere they need to go, except in a direction of self-knowledge and understanding of what knowledge her or his community really needs in order to rise up and prosper as an independently thinking people. In many cases, it takes individuals so far away from the education they need that it becomes virtually impossible to move in that direction. We should add, though, that miseducation is not reserved for those who have participated in the college or university experience. It is a process that begins before the individual can officially enter the formal educational setting and is found throughout life, at all educational attainment levels, in all forms of media and all social institutions for those targeted before birth for failure or intellectual peripheralization. With miseducation, individual Afrikans become mindless clones of their eurocentric academic mentors, no longer thinking, no longer wanting to think as Afrikans. Unlike miseducation, which does teach an appreciation of learning, although wrongful learning, diseducation leads the individual to despise the very idea of learning itself. It causes us to not want to learn at all. Diseducation creates an anti-learning psychology within its victims that predisposes them to reject any information and study that requires them to go beyond what is required for basic survival or assimilation. Like miseducation, diseducation is a conscious, institutionalized process designed to make a people useless and even destructive toward themselves because they see no reason to want to learn. Diseducation is further related to miseducation in that it can be a direct outcome of the recognition

that the individual has been miseducated if one feels he or she has too great of a vested interest in the culture or institutions of those who miseducated him or her to suicidally move against them, if there is so much rage that it cannot be corralled and focused toward rejection of the miseducation, or if one feels that he or she has gone too far down the miseducation road to recover from it.

52. Baruti, *Notes Toward Higher Ideals*, pp.32-34 and Baruti, *Homosexuality and Effeminization*, pp.424-432.

53 . Asafo is the Twi word for warrior. For a detailed explanation see Baruti, *Asafo* and the abridged definition of this term in an essay by the same name in Mwalimu K. Bomani Baruti, *Mentacide and other essays*, Atlanta, GA: Akoben House, 2005, pp.147-151.

54. Kwk stands for "katha wa katha" and is the KiSwahili term for etc. (et cetera) or "and so on." See the "Abbreviated Glossary" in the front of Kwame Agyei and Akua Nson Akoto, *The Sankofa Movement: ReAfrikanization and the Reality of War*, Washington, DC:)yoko InfoCom Inc., 1999.

55. The term euroversalization is a reconceptualization which more aptly than universalization describes what is going on culturally and socially in this world/reality. Instead of the politically   neutral,   blameless "universalize"/"universalized"/"universalizing," "euroversalize"/"euroversalized"/"euroversalizing" indicates the specific source and direction of this process. Universal locates its truths in the Universe, whether that be all that exists or the ourstorical evidence of normalcy in this planet's humanity. This is a deductive science, logically inferring from that above to that below. Euroversal is the truth according to the imperatives and limits of the european mind. It is an inductive science, extrapolating from the limited to the unlimited. It operates based on the assumption that others' cultures are simply deviations of one norm, theirs. And although some warrior scholars prefer the term globalization over universalization, for all intents and purposes they are the same. They are one in the same generic

macro process of imperialistic geographical, cultural and religious conquest and empire building through the supplantation of one people's way over that of all others for purposes of unmitigated exploitation. However termed, in their mind, this process leads to only one desired end for european people – global domination with the consent of the systematically oppressed noneuropean. For this reason and the fact that Europeans are this reality's imperialists, we will use the political reconceptualization of euroversalization to identify this process.

56.   This is not a derogatory use of the word "black," as we historically find in eurosupremacist thought, but a use that implies a void.

57.   This is not traditional Afrika and we cannot operate on the assumption that discussions arise out of a common understanding of truth and reality. Yes, in such an environment debate goes on until there is consensus. But, again, this is not then and we are not there. There is not a common understanding of who we are and what liberation and sovereignty mean among Afrikan people in this time and place. Therefore, we would be foolish to act as if there is.

58.   Laini Mataka, "It's All Right To Let Some People Into Yr Vestibule, But Never In Yr Livingroom," in Laini Mataka, *Never As Strangers*, Baltimore, MD: W.M. DuForcelf, 1988, p.14.

59.   It could not be absolutely impervious because Afrikans coming into themselves must have a means to enter.

60.   See "negroes" essay in Mwalimu K. Bomani Baruti, *negroes and other essays*, Atlanta, GA: Akoben House, 2000, pp.143-173.

61.   Larry D. Crawford (Mwalimu A. Bomani Baruti), "Racism, Colorism and Power," in Crawford (Baruti), *negroes and other essays*, pp.115-142.

62.   *Two Thousand Seasons*, Popenguine, Senegal: PER ANKH, 2000 (first published in 1973), p.24.

63.   Medase Nana Kofi Sechi for helping us overstand that we are rising out of those who came before us and therefore should refer to all who came into this physical reality through them should be referred to as "ascendants" and not "descendants."

64.   Baruti, *Eureason*, pp.113-114.

65.   Medase Mama Atiba.

66.   [Rhetorical ethic is a term Marimba Ani uses to characterize the European's] shameless, systematic, historical use of lies (false words) against others. These lies are intentionally designed to destroy others (true intent) through using their belief in the humanity of all humans to manipulate them into believing that Europeans are not trying to destroy them. It is the politics of morality, not universal morality, which rules. And in the Western cultural context, morality is purely political....Extreme individualism removes the possibility of a moral base, especially in Western culture, because anything that produces a profit or physical pleasure is morally correct. Regardless of the truth of an individual's statement, convincing others of its truth is what is most important. Skill at manipulating others' minds is the ultimate priority. Truth itself is irrelevant. It is set by the winner. So rules are meant to be broken. And because winning is everything, and deception the easiest and surest way to winning in Western society, there can be no moral rules except those arbitrarily given by the winner. It is the master of the lie who wins. For a lie is only a lie when one is caught. (Mwalimu K. Bomani Baruti, *The Sex Imperative*, Atlanta, GA: Akoben House, 2002, pp.204-205)

67.   Baruti, "negroes."

68 .   The Council on Black Internal Affairs, *The American Directory of Certified Uncle Toms*, NY: The Council on Black Internal Affairs, 2002, p.17.

69.   Even though given ourstorical knowledge, deteriorating contemporary conditions and the escalation of their ability to utilize their allocated influence, those who do not consciously act against us in service to others, who, by default, are not defined as

negroes, are to be dealt with as Nunu did Noble Ali in Haile Gerima's cinematic masterpiece *Sankofa* until he regained his revolutionary, nationalist consciousness.

70. See endnote 63.

71. Baruti, *Asafo*, p.42.

72. Mwalimu K. Bomani Baruti, *Yurugu's Eunuchs*, Atlanta, GA: Akoben House, 2009.

73. Mwalimu K. Bomani Baruti, "Self-Serving Spirituality" in Mwalimu K. Bomani Baruti, *Mentacide and other essays*, Atlanta, GA: Akoben House, 2005.

74. In the western reality, vices are so much easier to practice and lose oneself in than virtues. Like healthy relationships, virtues require hard, honest work. Vices, on the other hand, are open to even the weakest of people. A mind without sound cultural roots is easily twisted by the questions and "facts" others pose in defense of their so-called humanity. "A mind attacked and conquered is guided easily away from the paths of its own soul" (Ayi Kwei Armah, *Two Thousand Seasons*, Oxford, England: Heinemann, 1979, p.28). So, even in understanding that Europeans, as indicated by all of their history, are genoculturally evil, some would still argue that we are all made out of the same human genetic matter. They would have us believe that, even if Europeans are more evil, it is only because of accidental conditions of their arbitrary environmental "cradle." They would have us believe that it is no more than a result of having evolved in a different, cruder, much more savage environment than others. This eureason would have us believe, if we decide them guilty beyond reasonable doubt, that the way they are is not their fault and, therefore, it is the mission of those who recognize their fault for what it is to help them correct it. How different is this, outside of the more generalized and genetic component, from the subservient christian mentality embraced by so many Afrikans? It still keeps them at the center of our recovery as human beings. And, regardless, the result and permanent solution are the same for

us. It is not a matter of blaming them. It is a matter of understanding that they are to blame. By no means are they, now or then, innocent. If it were not for them, we would not have reason for being angry at each other for what we have allowed to happen to us. Simply put, it is a matter of them starting it and us finishing it. That's how warrior scholars, those revolutionary, uncompromising souls who are keenly aware that their people have been unjustly attacked, think *and act*. "Reasoning is the shackle of the coward" (Tamashek proverb). "A multitude of words cloaks a lie" (Hausa proverb). "We do not need to talk too much about it. That will harm the struggle" (Stokeley Carmichael (Kwame Toure), Pan-Africanism – Land and Power, *The Black Scholar*, Vol.27, No.3/4, 1998). The history of the relationship between Afrikans and Europeans should tell us that forgetting and forgiving do not even deserve a momentary reflection. It is a lie that not forgiving guilty people gives them power over you. They will hold power over you until you remove them from being in the position to unobstructedly wield their power over you. As long as they remain in that dominant position over you, your forgiveness of them is worthless in preventing them from destroying you and all that you represent. "If a fight is not yet spent, one does not intervene to end it" (Yoruba proverb). In fact, undeserved forgiveness gives them even more freedom to do against you what they will. If we look at the world through the revolutionary lens our Ancestors have bestowed upon us, we will see that the lie that forgiveness releases us from others' power over us only works for those who could not carry the weight of a warrior scholar's spirit anyway. In any truly egalitarian situation, in order for forgiveness to be sincerely granted, at minimum, these five invariable conditions must be met. The perpetrator(s) must:

(1) with the offended fully cognizant of their historical record of veracity, honestly ask for forgiveness. They must apologize, fully admitting that they have done what they have done. When the act was of a people, this apology must come from them as a people. What difference is the apology of a few when the act was collective? Yes, some of them may realize what they have done from their position of privilege, misguided liberalness and/or neediness, but, how is that relevant to us in the midst of our destruction?;

(2) have completely stopped committing the offensive (physical or mental) act;

(3) have stopped trying to draw comparisons between their crimes and those of their victims in an attempt to lessen the impact of what they did (as a schoolyard bully cries that he, too, was hit, as if that hit was not a provoked reaction to unwarranted, repeated aggressions);

(4) fully compensate the offended for the immediate pain and suffering, as well as that which was brought about by the offense(s); and

(5) have had their "blood debt" collected by those whose blood they needlessly wasted.

None of these apply to Europeans with respect to Afrikans. You apologize for what you truly feel bad about having done and actively seek to make amends for, give restitution to, repair the damage done. You do not just pretend that what you did has no meaning, or has produced an uncorrectable effect and, therefore, you cannot and are under no obligation to do anything about it. You *know* you are wrong and act accordingly. Forgetting, of course, is even more nonsensical because forgetting leaves one open for repeated assaults, by the same people, in the same way. Even worse, if you forget your way home, if you forget the destruction which brought you to where you are now, you will not be able to retrace your steps and reverse the process. You will not be able to find your way home. So, even if we rediscover our roots but do not understand what tore us from them, we can easily be ripped from them again and again and again, each time becoming more distant from the possibility of a full and final return. Forgetfulness can be even worse than forgiveness. Sadly, some of us see erasing any non-european sanctioned ourstorical truths and any ongoing atrocities against Afrikan people as critical to sustaining a mentacide we have accepted as our natural state of being. Those Afrikans openly advance an unqualified forgiveness and forgetfulness for the demonic attacks of europeans against us. In fact, blended with a "we're all human" argument, they argue that yurugu's penchant for creating havoc and pain must be euroversalized so that their peculiarly aggressive way will not arm those of us with the potential for consciousness with one of the critical tools we need to rightly set

Europeans apart from others so we can see them for what they are – genocultural self-remembrance. This is why these misguided individuals are so accepting of european liberal humanitarians who indicate that they are willing to apologize, forget the past and move on as one. They have found their ideal political mates – an apparently repentant enemy who wants nothing more than their attention, love and appreciation and, in turn, is willing to give them what they so desperately desire, their validation and defense against those of their own who would hold them accountable for their willful treason. To the mentacidal Afrikan made into the stunted shadow of a European liberal humanitarian, this is the ultimate victory.

75 . Amos N. Wilson, *The Falsification of Afrikan Consciousness*, Bronx, NY: Afrikan World InfoSystems, 1993, p.17.

76. Studied nonobservance is the term used to describe words or acts which people consciously ignore because they are considered abnormal or unbefitting of a given situation and do not warrant attention or which would create unnecessary embarrassment and/or discomfort if overtly given attention. For example, if family members are sitting around the dining room table eating a family dinner and the grandmother accidently flatulates, they will pretend not to hear or smell it, even though they obviously do.

77. Politico-economics (political economics) is the interaction of politics and economics. Primarily, it is the impact of competing political interests on the mobilization/accumulation/control of resources and their distribution among groups based on differentials of power and aggression. Higher studies for warrior scholars in this integrated concept can be found in Kwame Nantambu's *Decoding European Geopolitics: Afrocentric Perspectives*, Kent, OH: Imhotep Publishing Company, 1994 and *Egypt & Afrocentric Geopolitics*, Kent, OH: Imhotep Publishing Company, 1996.

78. Clarence J. Munford gives us an idea of the extent and contemporary continuity of this psychotic social pattern.

5,000 Blacks were crossing over annually by 1929 to "pass" for white. As of the year 1950, the defectors had soared to 12,000 per annum. By 1980 the yearly tally was 17,000. If that number held steady during the 1980s – conceivably it was greater – then during that decade alone, some 170,000 persons abandoned Black identity and the Black American community. Even a conservative estimate would place those who slipped away to pass for white in the sixty years from 1930 to 1990, at some 630,000. (*Race and Reparations: A Black Perspective for the 21st Century*, Trenton, NJ: African World Press, 1996, p.259)

79 . Afrikanity is a term descriptive of those qualities or characteristics which identify and define us as Afrikan. It is often used interchangeably with Afrikan centered, Africentricity or Afrocentricity.

80. Washington, DC: Pan Afrikan World Institute, 1992, pp.191-192.

81. Baba Baye Kes Ba Me-Ra also offers us a thoughtful contrast in his article "Two Types of Scholars in the Global African Community" (*Afrikan World Analysis*, July/October 2007, pp.4-5).

82. Cognitive dissonance is the psychology term used to describe the rationalizing response given by an individual who must settle for one thing when the more desirable one is unattainable. In this case, whatever settled for miraculously becomes defined as the better of the two and that which was most desired is pretended as being unwished-for and of lesser quality.

83. W.E.B. Dubois, *The Souls of Black Folk*, NY: Dodd, Mead & Company, 1961 (first published in 1903), p.3.

84. Baruti, Yurugu's Eunuchs, pp.87-93.

85. Akoto, *Nationbuilding*, pp.193-194.

86 . Kobi K.K. Kambon addresses this eureason within his discipline.

The traditional American psychology perspective interprets African behavior in terms of its deviation from a Eurocentric standard or norm....The comparative approach to African personality assessment assumes a cultural monistic conceptual base being predicated upon the so-called "melting pot" thesis. This thesis proposes that Africans in America and European-Americans are actually a homogeneous group. It views only the African experiential history of enslavement and the continuing experience of racial discrimination as perhaps mitigating/differentiating factors (along with the implicit assumption of inferior genetic condition). Therefore, it assumes equivalence of meanings and behaviors across obviously distinct cultural realities. (*The African Personality in America: An African-Centered Framework*, Tallahassee, FL: NUBIAN Nation Publications, 1992, pp.31-32)

87. Maafan is the adjective form of Maafa. Maafa is a KiSwahili term which refers to the entirety of the effort european people have put into trying to destroy the Afrikan continent, Afrikan culture and Afrikan people (even though its inception predates the systematic invasion of the Afrikan continent by Europeans by about 840 years when Arabs began their enslavement of Afrikans for themselves and exportation to China and other points in Asia). The european nation is our focus because they expended by far the greatest amount of energy aimed at bringing about our destruction. Ourstorically speaking, the Maafa is a massive, protracted "crime" against *our* humanity. In fact, to even use the word crime as descriptive of it severely minimizes the devastation it brought to Afrikan people. Holocaust is not even sufficient enough of a word. Be that as it may, the Maafa includes the unprovoked wars of invasion to capture and subdue the Afrikan continent, the violent dispersion of Afrikan peoples throughout it, the missionary efforts to remove us from our spirit, the consciously arrogant undermining of Afrikan cultural activities and sensibilities, the brutal and inhumane capture of Afrikans for enslavement and the removal of Afrikans to other lands, the colonization of Afrikan political systems, the balkanization of formerly peaceable ethnic groups and mass theft of Afrikan resources, the confiscation of Afrikan

lands and relegation of Afrikans to infertile soil, the global dehumanization of Afrikans, and the brutalization, rape, torture and murder of hundreds of millions of Afrikans and all the descendants those murdered individuals would have produced. It is important to note that most Afrikan centered warrior scholars recognize that the Maafa is a genocide in progress. It did not stop with the official end of our enslavement in the western hemisphere (noting that the enslavement of Afrikans on the continent by Arabs continues to date) or the termination of colonization on the continent through revolutionary warfare (noting that an advanced state of neocolonization still plagues virtually every Afrikan state). The continued efforts of white supremacist society to terrorize Afrikans into nonexistence and the ongoing psychological effects of our past enslavement (referred to by various terms such as psychic trauma, post-traumatic slavery syndrome, cultural misorientation, mentacide, kwk.), as well as the ongoing ruination of the Motherland under a heartless alien and alienating, paternalistic, capitalistic imperialism, are clear indicators that this has been and continues to be one, indivisible "Great Destruction." We must emphatically note, however, that this definition is not to imply that this atrocity is near completion. On the contrary, it is to provide the broadest picture and give a clear understanding of what happened, and is happening, so that conscious Afrikan people will understand the magnitude of what we have committed ourselves to reverse and, in the process, the traditions and sanity to which we fully intend to return.

88. There can be no oppressionless world where europeans and other oppression-bound people and their minions live. Many deluded to mouth this idealism in an innately evil reality want no more than to jump onto the eradicate oppression bandwagon because of their pressing desire to be uncritiqued for their inability (though usually unwillingness) to divest themselves from the european ways to which they have succumbed.

89. Yoruba proverb.

90. This last sentence is in reference to Listervelt Middleton's poem "The Charge" wherein he incisively remarks that "...no man

or woman that is free to chase stars is satisfied with chasing a ball..." (in Asa G. Hilliard, *African Power*, Gainesville, FL: Makare Publishing Company, 2002, pp.55-57)

91 .	Kwame Agyei and Akua Nson Akoto, *The Sankofa Movement: ReAfrikanization and the Reality of War*, Washington, DC:)yoko InfoCom Inc., 1999, p.233. Also see pp.8-10 for a detailed description of "the three phases of the reAfrikanization process" which are "Rediscovery, Redefinition and Revitalization."

92.	John Henrik Clarke.

93.	Odwira is pronounced ah-'dri-duh.

94.	Akan proverb.

95.	Baruti, "Evolutionary Science."

96.	Marimba Ani.

97.	Yoruba proverb.

98.	Marimba Ani, *Let the Circle be Unbroken*, New York, NY: Nkonimfo Publications, 1997, p.21.

99.	Ewe proverb.

100.	Marimba Ani makes a cogent statement about how we are used against ourselves in service to our destroyers.

> When a force is used against the people who create it instead of in their interests, the enemy is successful. This is the essence of good military strategy; the neutralization of the antagonist's force and then the use of that force to immobilize, to destabilize its source. That is what we have allowed our enemies to do. They study our tastes, create products which will appeal to us, then profit from our consumption of these products, and use them to retard the development of our consciousness, to keep us asleep. Our children buy gold objects from people who despise them;

objects made of gold which has been mined by the enslavement of their brothers and sisters. They buy the objects because Afrikans love to adorn themselves, as adornment touches and enhances the spirit. Our spirit is, in this way, used against us; its use is corrupted. The adornments touch the spirit, but they do not guide it in an Afrikan-centered manner. ("Kuugusa Mtima: The Afrikan 'Aesthetic' and National Consciousness," in Erriel Kofi Addae, *To Heal A People*, Columbia, MD: Kujichagulia Press, 1996, p.110)

101. Dona Richards, "European Mythology: The Ideology of Progress," in Molefi Kete Asante and Abdulai Vandi (eds.), *Contemporary Black Thought*, Los Angeles, CA: Sage Publications, 1985. This idea, erroneously connecting technical change with progress, is best expressed in the words of Marimba Ani (fka Dona Richards) thusly:

The white self-image requires an "inferior" to which it relates as "superior." The idea of progress helps to explain to Western-Europeans in what way they are "superior." They believe, and are able to make others believe, that since they represent the most "progressive" force at any given moment, they are most human and therefore "best." Others in the world represent varying degrees of inferiority....In this way, European culture...is made to be superior not only to what precedes it – as does its own past – but also to coexistent "unprogressive" cultures. In other words, the idea of progress provides a scale on which to weigh and by which to compare people via their cultures (their group creations). The Western-European ethos requires a self-image not merely of superiority but of *supremacy*, and the idea of progress makes white people supreme among human beings. It is superiority placed into the dimension of lineal time, and then the logic of lineal time placed into a timeless dimension. Without the idea and this conceptual sleight of hand, cultures would merely be different; Western culture would merely be intensely and obsessively rational. *With* the assumption of the idea of progress, the West becomes "better."....Technology provides the model of "efficiency," a model which more perfectly than anything imaginable concurs with the philosophy of change – for, in the European view, there is no end to efficiency either. No matter how effectively a machine may perform its function, it can always be made more effective and thereby a "new" and "better" machine. Progress is, in this way, "proven," and Western-Europeans can be said to "advance" as technology advances. (pp.64-65)

Also see "Evolutionary Science" in Baruti, *Eureason*, pp.53-62.

102. "Evolutionary Science" in Baruti, *Eureason*, pp.53-62.

103. Yoruba proverb.

104. Armah, *Osiris Rising*, p.110.

105. Deceit is but one negativity which needs to be dealt with in our Centers if we are to manage our relationships to our benefit in a peaceful, loving fashion. In general, the entirety of negotiating harmony among Afrikan warrior scholars is discussed by Fundi Sanyika Anwisye in his *The African Personality: Lubrication for Liberation: Can African People Get Along?: A Primer On Conflict Management* (St. Louis, MO: Blessings Not Curses Publications, 2007). It is a small book with enormous implications for interpersonal stability within the Afrikan community.

106. A. Hampaté Bâ, "The Living Tradition," in UNESCO General History of Africa (Vol.I), J. Ki-Zerbo (ed.), Berkeley, CA: University of California Press, 1981, p.172.

107. Undisputed Truth, "Smiling Faces."

108. Akan proverb.

109 . Eurisms are truths that Europeans have historically commonly accepted. While there are truisms that can be found to cross cultural boundaries, the body which is unique to Europeans, and usually in conflict with Afrikan truths, can be considered to be the central body of eurisms, since eurisms are conceptually used to illustrate fundamental cultural differences in perceptions of truth and untruth between Europeans and Afrikans. However, the entire body of eurisms includes both those that distinguish european truth from Afrikan truth and those of the vast majority of this world's indigenous peoples, present and annihilated by

Europeans.

110. Niccolò Machiavelli, *The Prince*, NY: Mentor, 1980 (first published in 1903).

111. Afrikan proverb.

112 . "The Book of Ankhsheshonqi" in Maulana Karenga, *Selections from The Husia*, Los Angeles, CA: The University of Sankore Press, 1984, p.65.

113. Igbo proverb.

114. My book *Nyansasem* is a worthwhile tool for this.

115. I would remind the reader of two things here. First, those Afrikans who completely mold themselves in Yurugu's image do so at a deeply psychological level. And this level is logically imitative of the entirety of Yurugu's personality, even those imperatives which operate at the asilic level. And, secondly, in Marimba Ani's relaying of the Dogon myth of Yurugu, we see that the European can never be complete, and this incompleteness will forever anger and frustrate him. This anger and frustration, though relatively less innately destructive, is carried as a blessing by those Afrikans who struggle to recreate themselves in his likeness.

116 . At the least, if not indisputable myths, they are not absolutes.

117. Yoruba proverb.

118. Asa G. Hilliard's sheepdog example of the method by which negroes are programmed to serve as yurugu's watchdogs is instructional (*The Maroon Within Us*, Baltimore, MD: Black Classic Press, 1995, pp.71-73).

119. Kamau Kambon, *The Last Book*, Raleigh, NC: 2005 and *Black Guerrilla Warfare In amerika*, 1983.

120. A poignant depiction of the horrific encounter between indigenous people and Europeans that every Afrikan family and school should have in its library is Jane Yolen's *Encounter* (NY: Voyager Books, 1992).

121. The record of this human atrocity is given us by Runoko Rashidi. Go to http://www.cwo.com/~lucumi/tasmania.html. Expand your search into his many other essays of ourstory on this site.

122. Afreason is the way of reasoning that is characteristically Afrikan. It is the cultural logic by which Afrikan thinking and speaking can be defined as originally Afrikan. It is both the thought and way of thinking that is uniquely Afrikan.

123 . Most of us became acquainted with this through its inclusion in the instructions during the rites of passage training for the boys in the television mini-series *Roots*. Regardless, knowing the propagandic agenda of western tell-lie-vision, we should be wise enough to question why certain lessons were selected over others.

124. Isfet is the state where, or period when, chaos reigns, when disorder is the norm. Isfet is considered to be the polar opposite of Ma'at, which exists when order rules.

125. Ma'at is the Kemetic goddess of universal harmony and justice. She also represents the principles of truth, righteousness, reciprocity, balance, order and propriety. As a force in the Universe, Ma'at is the progressive, generative spirit that constantly moves and organizes all life toward equilibrium within itself and in relation to others. The adjective Ma'atian refers to such a state. (See Jacob H. Carruthers, *Mdw Ntr: Divine Speech*, London: Karnak House, 1995 and Maulana Karenga, *Maat: The Moral Ideal in Ancient Egypt*, NY: Routledge, 2004.)

126. Relative to its numbers, any nationbuilding effort which cannot defend itself against aggressive, violent, persistent encroachments is unsophisticated and undeveloped.

127.   Yoruba proverb.

128.   Manu Ampim, *Towards Black Community Development*, Oakland, CA: Advancing the Research, 1993, p.31.   For the full discussion of this "commandment," read pages 31 through 34.

129.   Yoruba proverb.

130.   Mwalimu K. Bomani Baruti, "Subjective Objectivity," in Baruti, *Eureason*, pp.17-51.

131.   Richards, "European Mythology."

132.   Ibid, pp.136-137.

133.   Ethos refers to those aspects of a people's thought and behavior which make them unique.   It is the term used to describe the unique personality, made up of the unique collection of beliefs, sense of morality, sentiment and practiced character of a people, that distinguish them from others.   It can best be described as the personality or character of the culture.   Those definitions of ethos which are most applicable to what we are attempting to understand about ourselves, and others, here speak to a people's personality and culture as reflected in what they have done (their ourstorical, or historical, record) and what they are doing now and plan to do in the future, as measured in their eyes and those of others, usually as interpreted by them.   Maulana Karenga defines ethos as:

> ...the sum of characteristics and achievements of a people which define and distinguish it from others and gives it its collective self-consciousness and collective personality. (*Kawaida Theory*, Inglewood, CA: Kawaida Publications, 1980, p.90)

Significantly, he makes it understood that the quality of a people defined as their ethos is both thought and process, inextricably intertwined as an endless cycle of realization and struggle to greater realization.

> To know oneself is to grasp the essences of one's past, one's present and especially one's future possibilities and thereby

know who you are by what you have done and thus what you are capable of doing and becoming based on past achievement and current conditions. To produce oneself, is to create oneself through struggle against natural and social oppositions and through knowledge of what and who you can and ought to be. Thus, self-knowledge and self-production are at the heart of ethos and are clearly linked. For as a people struggles to overcome basic oppositions, then, it creates and defines itself and informs the world of its difference and distinctiveness, i.e., its ethos. Thus, *a people comes into being and knows itself by its achievements, and through its efforts to become and know itself, it achieves.* (Maulana Karenga, *Introduction to Black Studies*, Los Angeles, CA: Kawaida Publications, 1982, p.345)

134. Boston, MA: Northeastern University Press, 1989 (first published in 1931).

135. Kambon maintains that Severe CM is evident in Afrikans when

The European Survival Thrust is absolute and pervasive in the psyche [and there is] total allegiance to and reliance upon the European worldview....[while] there is little expression of any even subtle African psychological and behavioral tendencies or potentiality....This is manifested through such symptoms as hating Africanity/Blackness, and engaging in conscious-active hostility towards Blacks because of their Africaness (biologically-physically and behaviorally speaking) and/or towards things African (e.g., ideas, objects, etc.) in general. It is also manifested in prioritizing a social preference for associating with and even marrying non-Blacks, approving of and expressing violence toward other Blacks (for reasons other than self-individual-collective defense), including the killing of Blacks in the service or defense of Whites, and consciously and unconsciously working against the affirmation and self-determination of African people....Severe CM Africans cling so very tightly to the European worldview that they will sacrifice everything to uphold, maintain and defend its integrity within the African community and elsewhere. (*Cultural Misorientation: The Greatest Threat to the Survival of the Black Race in the 21st Century*, Tallahassee, FL: Nubian Nation Publications, 2003, pp.27-28)

He adds that such individuals are also prone to disfigure themselves according to european definitions of beauty and, in extreme cases, will manifest some of the most pathological european clinical psychological disorders. While this explanation is taken from Kambon's *Cultural Misorientation*, it is originally found in book form in his *The African Personality in America.*

136. Those Afrikans who operate at Kambon's Minimal CM level

> ...may in fact evidence a lot of anti-European or anti-Eurasian values, attitudes and behaviors along with the alien/Eurocentric and anti-Black tendencies that are basic to CM...they, nevertheless, evidence simultaneously a preponderance of European-centered beliefs, values, and attitudes in their functioning and behavior....They are probably more uncomfortable with African cultural identification than they are actually afraid of it, or anti-it, due to their acquired adaptation to the European worldview as a pseudo-normal psychological state of themselves. (Ibid. pp.25-26)

137. Kambon argues that most Afrikans are Moderately Culturally Misorientated.

> [They] evidence a variety of alien/Eurocentric and some anti-African tendencies, some conscious and some unconscious, through such symptoms as prioritizing racial integration with Whites (and other non-Blacks) in all aspects of life, and requiring White approval, recognition, affiliations and involvement to legitimize any activity of Blacks, holding a strong preference for Eurocentric cultural beliefs, values, rituals and customs, and see them (such principles and practices) as being as appropriate to Africans/Blacks in America as to Europeans/Whites in America....[They] see some legitimacy in Blackness so long as it ultimately seeks validation in integration or European/Eurasian affiliation (in actual or symbolic form). Thus, this group may actively seek a type of pseudo-African-centered affirmation, but through a European worldview framework....[They] interpret their Blackness in Eurocentric terms. (Ibid, pp.26-27)

138.   To some thinkers, this expansion of both the severely and minimally culturally misorientated, corresponding to a shrinkage of the number of those only moderately so, may be reminiscent of the rapid and disproportionate concentration of wealth at the top of the social hierarchy with a concomitant increase in those with less and less that typically foreshadows economic disaster in capitalist systems.   It may cause them to ask if this pattern speaks to a critical mass in self-hatred which may lead to implosion or explosion.

139.   Ibid, pp.64 and 67.

140.   Here we are speaking about the tail or tails most associated with the statistical model called a bell curve or normal distribution. A bell curve is a drawing representing the distribution of a population or group of people.   When it is normal, i.e., when whatever is being measured in the population or group, such as age, height, income, kwk, is normally distributed (those near the center being much more numerous than those at either the greater or lesser extreme), then, when it is drawn out in the form of a descriptive line, it resembles a bell in contour.   The center, or middle part, of the bell is where most of the people fit for whatever is being measured.   You can visualize how such a curve is statistically constructed utilizing an imaginary experiment.   Let's say that you were trying to find out what the age distribution of a given population looked like.   First you would use spray paint to write out, each about two feet apart in a straight row on a flat, level surface like a street, the ages in order from youngest to the oldest in this population.   Next, you would place a very tall glass wall, extending the length of this painted list, right beside this row for drawing the curve on later.   You would then, one at a time, begin to have the members of the population go and stand directly on top of the number which reflected their age.   If more than one person had the same age then the second to arrive would climb and stand directly on top of the fist arrival.   If there were a third, he or she would stand directly on top of the second and so on and so on until all of the individuals were standing, stacked in ladder fashion directly above the number of their ages.   And, finally, starting with the lowest age, on the glass wall you had erected beside this

lineup, you would use some bright colored chalk to draw a line from the top of the head of the highest person there to that of the highest person in the next number. You would continue this unbroken line from the top of one highest head to the next, sequentially, until a continuous line had been drawn across all the heads from the youngest to the oldest. Once that line was straightened (all the angles smoothed out) and all the people removed physically so that only the glass wall remained, what you would have before you would be the shape of the distribution of that population. (The same thing would occur if you had a building of the same number in floors as there were ages in the population and had an elevator on one side of the building that let each person off at his or her age-appropriate floor and then you drew a line around this outline once everyone on each floor was tightly lined up, front to back, in a row beginning at the elevator door; the only difference would be that you would be looking at the curve/distribution from another angle.) Among other things, that shape would tell you about among what ages there were more or less people relative to the whole population. It would reflect a distribution for that population, bell-shaped or not. A normal bell-shaped curve is presented in the drawing below, along with a skewed one. It is important for this discussion to know that some bell curves are asymmetrical (or "skewed"). This means that the distribution is lopsided, with more of the population concentrated at one extreme or the other, rather than the center (or what would ideally be considered the average). In fact, unlike normal or [fairly] symmetrical distributions where the average falls halfway between the highest and lowest possible values, asymmetrical distributions have averages which are often quite different than what should be expected, given normal curve expectations. But, back to the question of tails, the tails of a normal bell curve are found at the two ends, or extremes, where fewer and fewer people fall because these are the extremes. The tails fade out to nothing, as there are limits to the values of any variable (a variable being something in some way measurable which is found among different people, things or ideas of which there are different amounts or positions). The reader should note that only one of the distributions shown in the drawing on page 93 would be considered a fairly normal distribution. It is Kambon's Original

Estimate. According to this distribution, most Afrikans are what might be called average in their cultural misorientation, as the word moderate implies. Here, as in most normal distributions, we can see tails slightly tapering off at both ends of the curve. In his Amended Estimate, the average, in terms of where cultural misorientation is most concentrated among Afrikan people, is more equally divided between the Severe extreme and the Moderate average, leaving a fairly flattened out curve. Here, though, there are still tails at both ends. However, they are not so distinct, and the one at the Minimal Cultural Orientation end is the more obvious. My estimate of this distribution is an example of a moderately skewed distribution. The skew is found at the Severe extreme end of the cultural misorientation continuum which gives way to a more visible tapering tail interrupted by a considerable lump at its end.

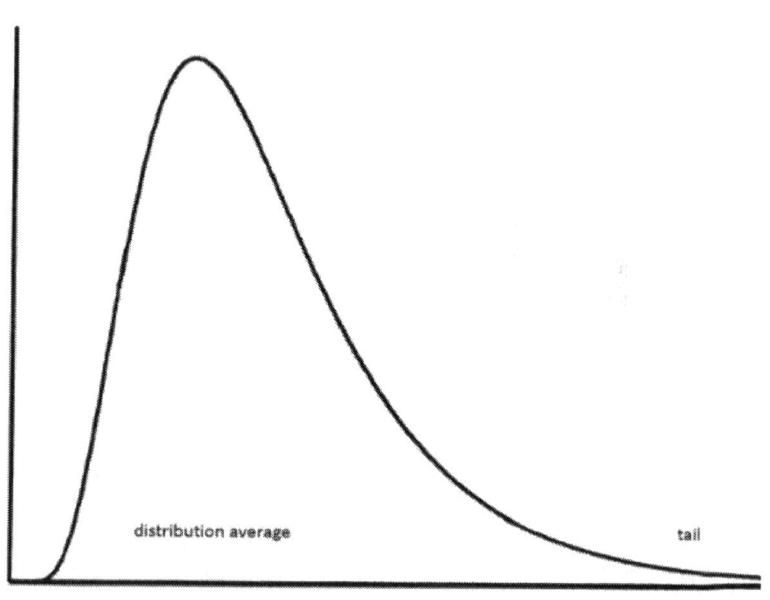

Skewed Distribution

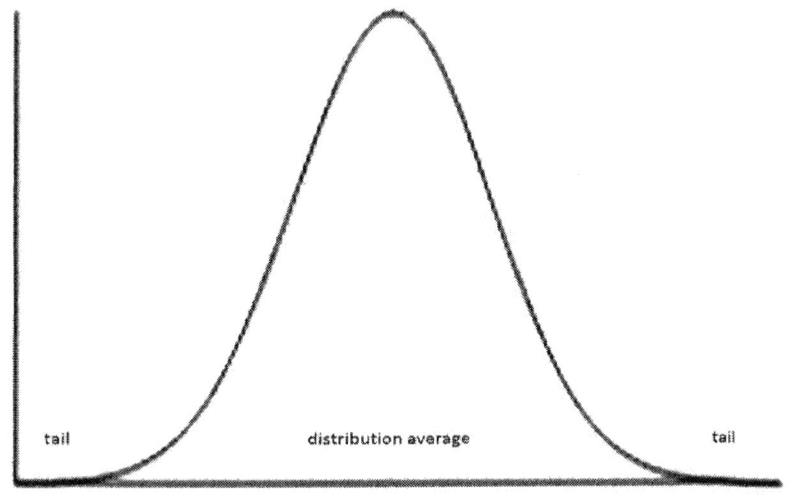

Bell-Shaped Distribution

141.   Ibid, p.25.

142.   The concepts "African Self-Extension Orientation" (ASEO) and "African Self-Concept" (ASC) help us see that the Afrikan does not abandon being Afrikan just because s/he has fallen into a chronic state of denial. No matter what the magnitude or nature of the european infection may be, no matter the degree of insanity, at the level of spirit there is no difference between Afrikans. The ASEO is the universal rhythm that is our Afrikan mind. It is the God force which shows us the Afrikan Way when we let it in to guide our thought and behavior. It is naturally, genetically connected to every fiber of our physical, mental and spiritual being because we are part and parcel of the Afrikan universe. It only requires acknowledgment to be tapped into. It is that inner self, that subconscious foundation that can lead us home to the harmony and order of the universe. With it, there is no loss, only gain. The ASC, on the other hand, is our individual understanding and manifestation of the ASEO. In a real way, it is its visible, outer self. The individual who peers back at us out of our mirrors is its

representative in this dimension. Here, individuals operate as selves who seem to independently and consciously act out what they believe to be their correct, or at least safe, human existence. But this conscious independence is not real, for we are not born, and do not grow or die, in a vacuum. Individuals interact with and are the product of the societal and cultural circumstances they find themselves a part of and influences that alter what should be normal thought and behavior. That does not necessarily mean social forces are beyond their control but, more often than not, they are beyond their consciousness. The ASC level of human thought is where the compromise of mind and spirit for Afrikans who find themselves subject to European asilic offenses takes place. Only at the ASC level can others' imperatives seep into and subvert our knowing, our truth, our empowering connection to the ASEO. Only at this level does cultural amnesia occur.

> ASC represents the conscious level expression/manifestation of the deepseated and unconscious ASEO. Thus, to speak of ASC, under normal-natural conditions, is to speak of ASEO. One dimension is encompassed by the other. To repeat, the "all-pervasive" ASEO is the foundation of ASC and they exist as a unified undifferentiated process merely having unconscious and conscious dimensions. (Kambon, *The African Personality in America*, p.59).

> Whatever may be the case for individual Africans...this model assumes that all African people possess this natural-innate disposition. It is simply more suppressed or inhibited in some of us (individually) than in others as a result of differential emphasis-reinforcement during early socialization experiences. Thus, the potential for the active manifestation of the basic African personality traits is everpresent in African people, and only its actual expression is subject to variability/modification in its occurrence. (Ibid, p.105)

The ASEO and the ASC are inseparable and inextricably intertwined. Even when the ASC is totally confused over where it should seek guidance and completion, the ASEO patiently and knowingly awaits its return as parents a prodigal child. It is through this explanation that we can see that the Afrikan reality and universe are always present, even when not consciously acknowledged. It is the individual who moves. What happens is that the ASC's influence is systematically suppressed at the conscious level by the imposition, and then voluntary internalization, of European thought and behavior. The natural ASC is denied when we are driven to be what we are not and should never desire to be. In order for any Afrikan to maintain the semblance of sanity when aping Europeans, the imprinting of their logic and way in his or her mind must become a self-rationalizing, self-sustaining process. It must lead those Afrikans to believe that thoughts and behaviors foreign to their spirit and way are naturally theirs. They must come to accept what is European as their essence. The European traits exhibited by confused Afrikans is much like the tarnish that will eventually completely discolor copper unless it is plated or cleaned and polished to brilliance. And similar to well-seasoned Afrikans, heavily weathered and tarnished copper gutters and roofs are often lauded as highly desirable, as the finished product of a beneficial chemical change. They both become culturally relative art forms that are considered as permanent, desirable states. Europeanized Afrikans who have gone through the europeanizing chemical changes in the corrosive vat of white supremacy have altered their ASC to the point that it cannot recognize its ASEO.

Although the two spheres are reversed in diagraming their model, Kwame Agyei and Akua Nson Akoto offer an excellent explanation of the two prominent aspects of the Afrikan self, although defined in terms of the earthly realities we must deal with, relative to the external environment and each other.

> The analogy of two concentric circles, where the core circle is the defining and primal reality, and the outer circle is peripheral and subordinate is applicable. The core of the Afrikan reality, and the ultimate focal point of our efforts, must be the restoration, development and maintenance of a sovereign, self sufficient and vibrant world Afrikan community, including its multitude of clans, ethnicity's, diasporan populations, regional associations, and nation-states. The major concern of the outer circle/sphere is the accommodation of a given Afrikan community to the political and economic exigencies of the peculiar political-economy in which it must interdigitate. As this outer sphere adapts or modulates the demands of the external order, it must do so in

a way that the continued viability and enhancement of the core sphere is facilitated. The role of this outer sphere must always be facilitating and never determinant. The relative priority of these two spheres must not be confused. (*The Sankofa Movement: ReAfrikanization and the Reality of War*, Washington, DC:)yoko InfoCom Inc., 1999, p.40)

143 .   Mwalimu K. Bomani Baruti, "Mentacide," in Baruti, *Mentacide*, pp.5-10.

144.   Kambon, *The Last Book.*

145.   That an addict (drugs, alcohol, sugar, salt, kwk) is "always" an addict and, therefore, must be on constant guard against contact with such substances, less they relapse, is an acknowledged fact within psychological circles.

146.   Here, density would be a measurement of the degree to which we remain able (capable) or willing to digest/listen to and learn from the logic of our Ancestors, knowing it will nullify our european addictions. It is a measure of our fortitude in resisting genocultural oppression. The greater the density, the less the alien access. The less the density, the more likely eureason can find fertile ground within which to plant itself. The range of the latter state is a measure of fluidity. It tells us of the degree of our lack of commitment to move in the Way of our Ancestors.

147.   This statement about just what should be meant by Afrikan progress in the face of this anti-Afrikan european reality is a modified version of the concluding chapter in my *Sesh: An Afrikan Centered Guide to Writing and Self-Publishing*, Atlanta, GA: Akoben House, 2007, pp.154-156. It bears repeating.

148.   Even being still is movement. We are always moving in some direction.

149.   Mwalimu K. Bomani Baruti, "Irreconcilable Differences," in Mwalimu K. Bomani Baruti, *Eureason*, Atlanta, GA: Akoben House, 2006, pp.201-241.

150 .   Ayi Kwei Armah, *Two Thousand Seasons*, Popenguine,

Senegal: PER ANKH, 2000 (first published in 1973), p.303.

151. *The Healers*, Popenguine, Senegal: PER ANKH: 2000 (first published in 1978), p.204.

152. Ibid, p.100.

153. Mwalimu K. Bomani Baruti, "Frustration Denied," in Mwalimu K. Bomani Baruti, *Battle Plan*, Atlanta, GA: Akoben House, 2006, pp.54-57.

154. Baruti, *Sesh*, pp.154-156 and Baruti, *Nyansasem*, p.11.

155. Akoto, *Nationbuilding*, p.182.

156. Armah, *Osiris Rising*, p.69.

157. Akan proverb.

158. Mwalimu K. Bomani Baruti, *Complementarity: Thoughts for Afrikan Warrior Couples*, Atlanta, GA: Akoben House, 2004, p.14.

159. Molefi Kete Asante, *Afrocentricity*, Trenton, NJ: Africa World Press, 1988, p.54.

160. Yoruba proverb.

161. Akan proverb.

162. Afrikan proverb.

163. An egogenic society is one which automatically breeds needy, selfish, hedonistic individuals and does this in inordinate numbers. This innate imperative and propensity is very similar to what Amos N. Wilson in his *Understanding Black Adolescent Male Violence* calls "crimogenic" society, which breeds unusual numbers and types of criminals and a relatively high level of crime and violence (NY: Afrikan World InfoSystems, 1992, p.6). An Afrikan interpretation of society's responsibility for criminal

behavior among its citizens is well articulated in Kimbwandènde Kia Bunseki Fu-Kiau's *African Cosmology of the Bântu-Kôngo: Principles of Life & Living* (Brooklyn, NY: Athelia Henrietta Press, 2001 (first published in 1980), pp.73-75).) This is also comparable to a society's responsibility to the production of excessively-developed egos.

164. In many ways, friendship is no less a struggle than complementarity and/or marriage.

165. At the lowest levels of everyday survival of my people, I feel despair tug at my heart every time a Brother or Sister on the street asks me for a dime, a piece of a meal, a hand to shake in recognition that they are not invisible. Every Afrikan, who is Afrikan at heart, should [feel compelled to] do something concrete about whole human beings recast in the image of lone insects, scavenging for food, drugs and whatever else to which their vision has been reduced.

166. The Zanzibar Revolution masterminded by John Okello (*Revolution in Zanzibar*, Nairobi, Kenya: East African Publishing House, 1967), Robert Charles stand against a frenzied mob of 20,000 lynchers (Munford, *Race and Reparations*, p.217) and the Haitian Revolution which permanently scarred yurugu's ego (Jacob H. Carruthers, *The Irritated Genie*, Chicago, IL: The Kemetic Institute, 1985) are but a few of the examples of us rising and winning against all odds.

167. Commodores, "Heroes."

168. One other definite conclusion can be drawn from the collective revolutionary experience about the initial meetings that take place between two potential complements that lead to the development of lasting warrior relationships. They both tend to be doing their work when they first meet. This does not mean that they are oblivious to the need for companionship. It only means that finding a mate is not their sole priority or an overriding focus. Therefore, using this pattern as a guide, if you are doing your work, your study, your communal involvement, your communicating, attending to the needs of our people as a nation, your complement will

be there also. You will find each other. Let your example be your attraction. (Baruti, *Complementarity*, p.14.)

169. "Godless Reason" in Baruti, *Eureason*, pp.63-109.

170. In our oral tradition "nommo" is power. It is a force activated of thought and word. Thoughts manifest in language create reality. Words give ideas power. Yet nommo is not just "creative visualization." Nommo is spoken reality, thought spoken, thought creating truth. It is more than just spoken words, for some things do not have to be said. They are known and understood. However, in order for nommo to exist among a people, there cannot be a contradiction between the laws of the universe, what they say and what they do. In this respect, language in western society cannot be defined as nommo because it is not an expression of truth. Language is seen as a tool to be mastered in order to trick others. In its written and oral forms, it is a political instrument designed to gain leverage and control over others in order to dominate them in the midst of confusion. Language in european culture is purely political. It is primarily for the purpose of producing and controlling a beneficial, superior European image and the use of that illusion to dominate others. In our oral tradition "nommo" is power (Jacob H. Carruthers, *MDW NTR Divine Speech: A Historiographical Reflection of African Deep Thought From The Time of The Pharaohs to The Present*, London: Karnak House, 1995, A. Hampaté Bâ, "The Living Tradition," in UNESCO General History of Africa (Vol.I), J. Ki-Zerbo (ed.), Berkeley, CA: University of California Press, 1981, pp.166-203, Janheinz Jahn, *Muntu: African Culture and the Western World*, NY: Grove Weidenfeld, 1990 (first published in 1958), p.27).

> Nommo seeks to conceptualize the ability to activate....It is more, even, than the spoken word. Nommo often takes these forms, but its essence resides in the activating energy that *makes use of* the forms. Nommo can be thought. Nommo can be played on an instrument. Nommo can be sung. It is prayer. It is curse. It is incantation! Nommo is a praise song. Nommo is our use of the spiritually activating principle. Nommo is will and intent. Nommo is consciousness. (Ani, *Let the Circle be Unbroken*, p.40. Also

see Jahn, *Muntu*, pp.121-155.)

171.   "Asase Yaa" is the Twi name for Mother Earth.

172.   Jacob H. Carruthers, *Intellectual Warfare*, Chicago, IL: Third World Press, 1999, pp.42-49.

173.   Again, flora and fauna made endangered by noneuropeans have been the direct result of european driven interests or are the consequence of their direct or indirect exploitation by Europeans.

174.   Zoophobic means fear and hatred of animals.

175.   Herbaphobic means fear and hatred of vegetation.

176.   Geophobic means fear and hatred of planet Earth.

177.   Anthrophobic means fear and hatred of humanity or human beings. Interestingly, this fear and hatred of life has led this people to love and worship machines. It is in their company where they are the most comfortable. They would like nothing better than to dispose of their biological shells and have their spiritless essence be deposited in robotons.

178.   Biophobic means fear and hatred of life.

179.   Akan proverb.

180.   Sam Yette, *The Choice*, Silver Spring, MD: Cottage Books, 1971, p.100.

181 .   This sentiment, and the mentality behind it, found universally across the Afrikan continent, is summarized quite well by Kimbwandende Kia Bunseki Fu-Kiau in his *African Cosmology of the Bântu-Kôngo*, pp.64-69.

182.   It is interesting that, in western language, soil carries negative denotations and connotations, i.e., to make dirty, as in unclean or pollute, defile, corrupt.

183.   In a strange way, Europeans recognized this in the myth of Antaeus, the titan who could only be defeated once he was physically separated from his mother Earth. Of course, others, more astute in eureason, would argue that this was no more than a lesson of war, where an individual/people is better defeated when their source of power is identified and they can be separated from it.   Some might even argue that this is symbolic (a coded reference) of the genocidal war strategy of Europeans against Afrikan people.

184.   *The Usual Suspects.*

185.   See endnote 38.

186.   Kikuyu proverb.

187.   E. Bólájí Ìdòwú, *Olódùmarè: God in Yorùbá Belief*, New York, NY: Wazobia, 1962, p.156.

188.   *The Falsification of Afrikan Consciousness*, pp.44-45.

189.   When it comes down to the personal risk involved in being Afrikan in a place where people will try to financially hurt you simply because you are acting on that choice, ask yourself whether the Creator and the Ancestors have ever allowed your basic needs not to be met.

190.   Armah, *Osiris Rising*, p.261.

191 .   The Black Dot deftly analyzes this relative to the exploitation of our youth in the despiritualized western music business in *Hip Hop Decoded* (NY: MOME Publishing Inc., 2005).

192.   It is interesting on this point of mentality to note the words of a Malian contemporary, Yaya Diallo, who relates that

> ...the African climate does not allow laziness. If we do not
> learn at home to exert ourselves physically and mentally,

nature will be hard on us. If we do not accept suffering along the way, we will be unreconciled to life. (*The Healing Drum: African Wisdom Teachings*, Rochester, VT: Destiny Books, p.17)

Among the Chagga, we find a remarkably similar longstanding sentiment. Their sages maintain that

Mediocrity and averageness are despicable enemies of the indigenous worker...Everyone strives to do their best. (R. Sambuli Mosha, *The Heartbeat of Indigenous Africa*, NY: Garland Publishing, Inc., 2000, p.138)

193. Carruthers, *Intellectual Warfare*, pp.35-42.

194. This point is eloquently made by Julius K. Nyerere in his essay "Ujamaa – The Basis of African Socialism" (*Ujamaa – Essays on Socialism*, NY: Oxford University Press, 1968, pp.1-12).

195. Elleni Tedla, *Sankofa: African Thought and Education*, NY: Peter Lang, 1995, p.32, Anthony Ephirim-Donkor, *African Spirituality: On Becoming Ancestors*, Trenton, NJ: African World Press, 1997, pp.108-110 and Kwame Gyekye, *African Philosophical Thought: The Akan Conceptual Scheme*, Philadelphia, PA: Temple University Press, 1995, pp.154-162.

196 . Amos N. Wilson, *The Falsification of Afrikan Consciousness*, NY: Afrikan World InfoSystems, 1993, pp.45-55 and *Blueprint for Black Power: A Moral, Political and Economic Imperative for the Twenty-First Century*, NY: Afrikan World InfoSystems, 1998, pp.731-740 and Ivan H. Light, *Ethnic Enterprise in America*, Los Angeles: University of California Press, 1972.

197. This is critical for Afrikan warrior scholars to understand. It might be different if this threat were new or unknown to us. But we are well versed in the way of Europeans. Nothing coming from them should surprise us, nothing. So, the idea of discussions about the nature or magnitude of the threat makes no sense, whether we are able to visibly perceive it at this particular

moment or not.

198.   Http://www.youtube/watch?v=LU8DDyz68kM.

199.   *African Spirituality: On Becoming Ancestors*, Trenton, NJ: Africa World Press, 1997, p.45.

200.   Fihankra is an Adinkra symbol of the Akan people of West Afrika which means safe area.

> Fi-hankare is suggestive of one type of Ghanaian architecture or building style that the Akan prefer.   That basic style consists of a central quadrangle which is enclosed on all four sides with rooms.   The basic concept and theory typifies protection against outside elements and, therefore, suggests security and solidarity....**Fi-hankare** (a traditional home design) represents brotherhood and solidarity because a house is a safe and secure place.   The Akan place high value on the strength of family ties and family groups.   To Ghanaians, a four-sided home in the form of a quadrangle represents safety and security....The concept and design of *fi-hankare* seen from the air reveals a house with four sides and a compound in the middle.   This type of home, which is common throughout Akan society, represents physical protection and reinforces the idea of family unity, or the family coming together. (W. Bruce Willis, *The Adinkra Dictionary*, Washington, DC: The Pyramid Complex, 1998, pp.106-107)

201.   *Notes for an African World Revolution: Africans at the Crossroads*, Trenton, NJ: Africa World Press, 1991, p.7.

202.   A good place to start would be Balogun O. Abeegunde's *Afrikan Martial Arts: Discovering the Warrior Within*, Atlanta, GA: Boss Up, Inc., 2008.   I would also suggest reading books like Che Guevara's *Guerrilla Warfare*, George L. Jackson's *Blood in My Eye*, Kwame Nkrumah's *Handbook of Revolutionary Warfare*, V.I. Lenin's *Guerrilla Warfare* and William Powell's *The Anarchist Cookbook*.   Read these, interpreting them from an Afrikan center.   See what works and what is simply fluff for the excitable novice.   Go further.   Read the weapon and survival magazines.   Study the old boy scout and army survival manuals.

Read Octavia Butler's *Parable of the Sower* (ignoring the interracial confusion and the idea that a land deed bought now will be respected in any future without your enforcement under your government). A copy of the video *Alone in the Wilderness* might also prove useful.

203. Baruti, *Homosexuality and the Effeminization of Afrikan Males*, pp.149-150.

204. Teumari is the Amharic (Afrikan) term for what we mistakenly call mentees. As with Jegna, it carries a much deeper responsibility and character qualification than the homosexualizing eurocentric concept. It is pronounced tay-oo-mah-ree.

205. "From Na Ezaleli to the Jegnoch," in Lee Jones (ed.), *Making It on Broken Promises: African American Male Scholars Confront the Culture of Higher Education*, Herndon, VA: Stylus Publishing, 2002, p.181. Also see Elleni Tedla, *Sankofa: African Thought and Education*, NY: Peter Lang, 1995, p.67 and Asa G. Hilliard (Nana Baffour Amankwatia), *African Power*, Gainesville, FL: Makare Publishing Company, 2002, pp.18-21. Kwame Agyei Akoto gives a definition of "Mwalimu" (a KiSwahili term for teacher) which, although it focuses almost exclusively and very extensively on the role of an authentic Afrikan educator, is inextricably tied to that of "Jegna."

> That individual who assumes the role of mwalimu, or who is so appointed, must be one who is not only studied in the history and culture of our people, but one who is in complete identification with it. The mwalimu must not only be involved in the study of the culture, but must be involved in a concrete and ongoing way with advancing the cultural and/or political interests of Afrikan people. The mwalimu comes before his wanafunzi (students) as a representative of the whole culture. The mwalimu is entrusted with the task of inculcating the essential values of that culture and thereby guaranteeing its continuation. The mwalimu comes to the classroom representing in one sense the limitations of tradition and the existing order. The mwanafunzi comes to the classroom representing the new order or unlimited potentiality. The mwalimu, as a representative of the current

order, brings with him/her all the accumulated wisdom of tradition and must seek to impart that wisdom in a way that inspires and fuels the new energy and unlimited potential of mwanafunzi. The mwalimu must possess a general command of that accumulated wisdom, along with a specific mastery of a chosen area of specialty. Beyond that general competence, the mwalimu must possess a deep-felt and infectious drive to achieve greater command of both the wisdom of tradition and modernity....The mwalimu can only be effective in fulfilling that task if he/she is an active participant in that working collective that is devoted to the cultural, political and economic development of the Afrikan community. The mwalimu must bring enthusiasm, conviction, ideological clarity, moral integrity, and courage, as well as knowledge, to the teaching/learning environment. The latent messages and information shared by the mwalimu through physical nuance, voice pattern and tone, hair style, dress, and character are as important to the effective teaching/learning environment as the structured lessons. If the mwalimu is deficient in either area, the respect of the wanafunzi, and the efficacy of the teacher/learner encounter will be compromised. Given the critical role that the mwalimu must play in the maintaining and enhancing the national culture, it is no wonder that in classical Afrikan civilizations and in still viable traditional societies, the higher or core knowledge was entrusted only to its most esteemed elders and spiritual leaders. (*Nationbuilding: Theory & Practice in Afrikan Centered Education*, Washington, DC: Pan Afrikan World Institute, 1992, pp.99-100, although the entire subchapter on "Who: The Character of the Mwalimu" on pp.99-104)

206. Nana and Elder are earned titles. Titles of good character, given by people of good character, are of a deserved prestige, honor and privilege. The titles of Nana and Elder speak to those Afrikans of demonstrated character, of strong, proven character, a jegna's character. The making of such a character is inconsistent with people "buying" such honors on the Continent, though it does fit the western mentality of the unfit purchasing titles through their ill-gotten gains, of which the Nobel Peace Prize is a prime example, having been bought by and named after the father of explosives in european history. So, when we look at those Afrikans (and Europeans) praising themselves for the titles they were awarded on the Continent, by people who, in many cases, did

not know them or their character, or only knew of a foreign reputation and what resources they had access to, we find little more than weak egos finding security in titles they did not earn but which place them above having their insecurities revealed. According to our traditions, all things (including our humanity), must be earned, continuously over a person's lifetime. Titles are bestowed by those who know you. They are not something you can arbitrarily claim for yourself in a vacuum or in the absence of clear, common evidence. The vast majority of Afrikans walking around this society boasting titles have not earned what they claim and the people "awarding" them these titles (which technically, based on the established criteria of having to have known these individuals, they do not have the right to do so) do not know them. Neither time nor condition changes the qualification of giver or receiver of titles. If this qualification for honor goes down, then the content of the character required for the honor also declines. And, if this were the way we had always bestowed titles of honor, then the substance of our culture and traditions would have to also always have been weak.

207. Ibid, p.76.

208. Wofa Kwasi Odaaku.

209. Akan proverb.

210 .   Afrisms are truths that Afrikans have ourstorically commonly accepted. While there are truisms that can be found to cross cultural boundaries, the body which is unique to Afrikans, and usually in conflict with european truths, can be considered to be the central body of Afrisms, since Afrisms are conceptually used to illustrate fundamental cultural differences in perceptions of truth and untruth between Afrikans and Europeans. However, the entire body of Afrisms includes both those that distinguish Afrikan truth from european truth and those which are generally shared by the indigenous peoples of the world.

211. KiSwahili proverb.

212. Ayi Kwei Armah, *KMT: in the house of life*, Popenguine, Senegal: PER ANKH, 2002, pp.194-195.

213. Yoruba proverb.

214. Amos N. Wilson explains the wholistic effect of possessing consciousness on the individual and/or group thusly:

> To possess consciousness is to be possessed by consciousness. For consciousness "takes over" and represents itself in the body as feelings, emotions, tastes, values, intelligence, and behavior. When relatively stable or consistent, habitual dispositions and tendencies which dynamically structure and are reciprocally structured by consciousness, incline the individual or group to act or react in certain fairly predictable ways....[Therefore], to shape and organize consciousness is to a measurable extent to shape and organize the mind and body as well as their behavioral deployment and expression. (*Blueprint for Black Power*, pp.86 and 87)

215. Akan proverb.

216. J.A. Sofola explains this ourstorical Afrikan characteristic well in his *African Culture and the African Personality* (Ibadan, Nigeria: African Resources Publishers, Co., 1973).

217. In general, power is the direct, unmitigated exercise of self-determining conscious thought, regardless of others' interests or interference. It is the uncompromised actualization of one's will into existence with the force that prevents any successful challenge to its determined presence. There is no questioning conscious, historically grounded, spirit-driven power. Influence, on the other hand, is not power. It is the attempt to alter another more powerful individual or group's opinion or action to your advantage. It is of a lesser breed. Sociologically speaking, one cannot exercise influence as a means of *forcing* one's will. Of the two, only power can be effectively exercised in this way. The exercise or threat of exercising power falls within the domain of power, not influence. Therefore, outside of the intervention of the influencer's charisma, which is unlikely to seriously impact those well trained in manipulation, influence is the act of

belief in chance. It is an expectation of a probability based on the good will, gullibility and/or objective humanity of power holders. In the case of Afrikans, relative to Europeans, it is an act of wishful hoping against the record of history. It is an attempt at a pretense that gives the illusion of integrity and substance to a voluntarily servile manhood. (Baruti, *Asafo*, p.16)

218. Baruti, *Asafo*, pp.15-36.

219. *A Great and Mighty Walk.*

220. Abibifahodie ('ah-bee-bee-fah-'hoe-dee-ay) is a Twi word being used to greet revolutionary Afrikans (as well as acknowledge sneezes, instead of saying "Bless you") in order to affirm regularly and as often as possible our victorious destiny.

221. To quote Amilcar Cabral, "Any action, regardless of its motives, is sterile unless it produces practical and concrete results."

222. Yoruba proverb.

Akoben House Order Form

Please send

_____ copies of *Sovereignty* ($19.95 each)	$ _____
_____ copies of *Clarity* ($21.95 each)	$ ___
_____ copies of *A Warrior's Love* ($16.95 each)	$ ___
_____ copies of *Message to The Warriors* ($19.95 each)	$ _____
_____ copies of *IWA: A Warrior's Character* ($24.95 each)	$ _____
_____ copies of *Centered* ($16.95 each)	$ _____
_____ copies of *Yurugu's Eunuchs* ($18.95 each)	$ _____
_____ copies of *Nyansasem: Revolutionary Daily Thoughts* ($19.95 each)	$ _____
_____ copies of *Sesh* ($16.95 each)	$ _____
_____ copies of *Eureason* ($19.95 each)	$ _____
_____ copies of *Notes Toward Higher Ideals in Afrikan Intellectual Liberation* ($16.95 each)	$ _____
_____ copies of *Battle Plan* ($14.95 each)	$ _____
_____ copies of *Kebuka!* ($18.95 each)	$ _____
_____ copies of *Mentacide and other essays* ($16.95 each)	$ _____
_____ copies of *Asafo* ($19.95 each)	$ _____
_____ copies of *Complementarity* ($18.95 each)	$ _____
_____ copies of *Homosexuality and the Effeminization of Afrikan Males* ($29.95 each)	$ _____
_____ copies of *The Sex Imperative* ($19.00 each)	$ _____
_____ copies of *Excuses, Excuses* ($17.00 each)	$ _____
_____ copies of *negroes and other essays* ($17.00 each)	$ _____
_____ copies of *Chess Primer* ($16.95 each)	$ _____

Shipping & Handling: $ _____

($6 for 1 book and $4 for each additional book.)

TOTAL ENCLOSED: $ _____

NAME: _____________________________________

ADDRESS: ____

Send this order form, along with your check or money order (made payable to Akoben Village), to:

Akoben House, P.O. Box 10786, Atlanta, GA 30310 OR order by credit card at

www.AkobenHouse.com

35963383R00128